MORE
MYSTERIES & MARVELS
OF
NATURE

INSECT LIFE
Dr. Jennifer Owen

REPTILE WORLD
Dr. Ian Spellerberg

BIRD LIFE
Ian Wallace

Contents

The material in this book is also available as three separate books:
Insect Life, **Reptile World** and **Bird Life**
in the Mysteries & Marvels series, published by Usborne.

First published in 1984 by Usborne Publishing Ltd, 20 Garrick Street, London WC2E 9BJ.

Copyright © 1984 Usborne Publishing Ltd.

The name Usborne and the device are Trade Marks of Usborne Publishing Ltd.

Printed in Great Britain

PART 1

MYSTERIES & MARVELS
OF
INSECT LIFE

Dr. Jennifer Owen

Edited by Rick Morris

Designed by Anne Sharples
and Teresa Foster

Illustrated by Ian Jackson
and Alan Harris

Cartoons by John Shackell

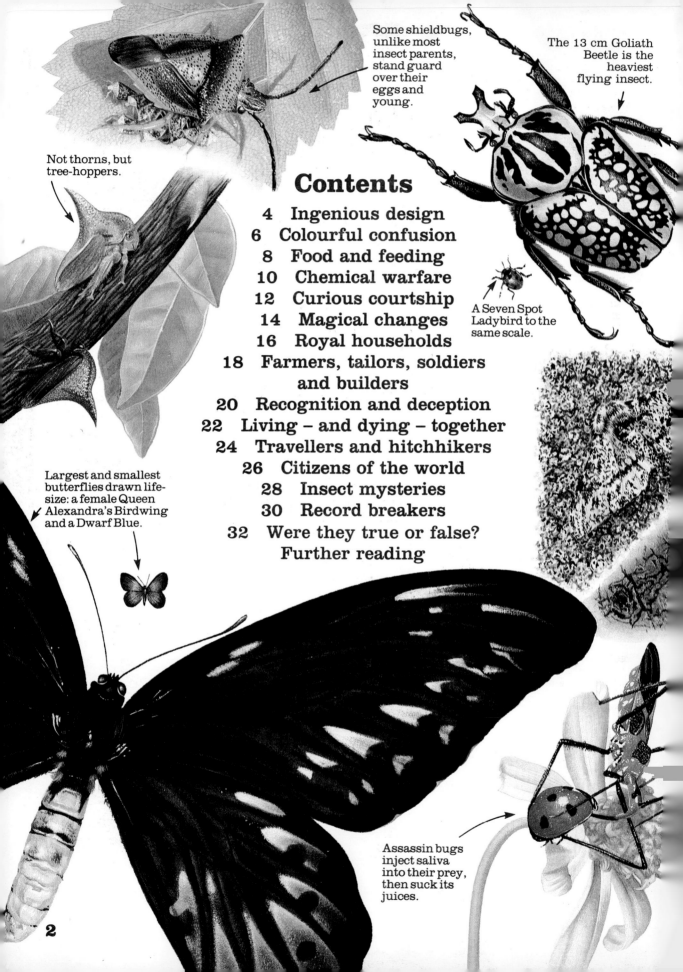

Some shieldbugs, unlike most insect parents, stand guard over their eggs and young.

The 13 cm Goliath Beetle is the heaviest flying insect.

Not thorns, but tree-hoppers.

Contents

A Seven Spot Ladybird to the same scale.

Largest and smallest butterflies drawn life-size: a female Queen Alexandra's Birdwing and a Dwarf Blue.

Assassin bugs inject saliva into their prey, then suck its juices.

Painted Ladies fly over 5,000 km from Africa to Britain.

A 12 mm click beetle can catapult to a height of 300 mm.

Well-camouflaged Peppered Moths: the dark form has developed where pollution blackens tree trunks.

An Ant-lion larva digs a trap for ants.

Ground level

A cutaway view of the trap

A leaf insect, complete with leaf-like marks and legs like twigs.

About this book

There are about a million species of insects and they outnumber all other sorts of animals by almost four to one. This book is a stimulating introduction to their extraordinary variety and abundance, and concentrates on the more curious and unexpected aspects of insect life.

Insects range in size from larger than the smallest mammals to those tiny enough to crawl through the eye of a needle. The following pages describe some of the ingenious structures and strategies that they use in staying alive — moving, feeding and defending themselves — and in reproducing their kind. The book looks at beetles that stick like limpets, blood-sucking moths, praying mantids that look like flowers, sawflies that vomit pine resin at attackers, the language of bees, and the link between poisons and colours.

An insect's body is in three parts and all insects have three pairs of legs. Some do not have a common name and are called by their latin-based scientific name.

This book will lead to an understanding of why insects are so successful but also points out that there is still much to be discovered about insects and the way they live.

TRUE or FALSE?

Look out for these questions and try to guess if they are true or false. The answers are on p. 32.

Ingenious design

The bodies of insects are amazingly varied in shape and form. All these designs are answers to the problems of moving, breathing, keeping warm, eating and avoiding being eaten.

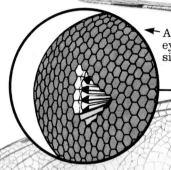

← A close-up of the eye showing the six-sided lenses.

Between the compound eyes are three small simple eyes which respond to light.

Aerial hunters ▶

The large second and third segments of a dragonfly's body are tilted, bringing all the legs forward below the jaws, where they form a basket for catching other insects in flight. Dragonflies strike with deadly accuracy, guided by the enormous compound eyes, each made up of as many as 30,000 separate lenses. Each lens reflects a slightly different view of the world.

Dragonfly hunting a butterfly.

Each foot has 5,000 bristles which end in pairs of flat pads.

Water-skiing

In an emergency, the rove beetle, *Stenus*, only 5 mm long, can zoom across the surface of water. Glands at the tip of the abdomen release a liquid that lowers the surface tension of water. The beetle is pulled forward by the greater surface tension of the water in front of it.

▼ A gripping story

When threatened, a tiny leaf-eating beetle, *Hemisphaerota cyanea*, can clamp down like a limpet. Just as water between two sheets of glass sticks them together, so the beetle uses a film of oil between the 60,000 pads on its feet and the leaf.

Ants heave unsuccessfully at the rounded "shell".

Hemisphaerota cyanea

There are over 40,000 species of weevil. They lay eggs in nuts, such as chestnuts, hickory and hazel, which the grub eats from the inside.

Antennae

Jaws

Elephant Weevil

All the colours of the rainbow

Butterfly wings are covered with tiny over-lapping scales. Iridescent colours result from the way some scales reflect light, and depend on structure not pigment. Other scales have colour pigments.

In this close-up of scales, the orange and deep purple ones have pigment colours. The iridescent blue and green scales have little pigment but reflect blue or green light.

Morpho butterfly

Two views of an iridescent wing. Colour depends on the light angle.

Scales increase "lift" when flying.

A boring story ▶

The jaws of weevils are at the end of a long snout which, in nut weevils, may be as long as the rest of the body. The tiny weevils bore holes in hard nutshells by using the snout as a lever to increase pressure.

Scuba diving and air lines

Some diving beetles use an air bubble trapped between their bodies and their wing cases for breathing under water. Oxygen from the water replaces some of the air used but slowly the bubble shrinks and the beetle must re-surface. Other insects have breathing tubes: the Rat-tailed Maggot's tube is telescopic.

The Water Scorpion has an air tube.

Some diving beetles tow an air bubble.

The Rat-tailed Maggot's tube is 27 cm.

TRUE or FALSE?

Bumblebees have central heating.

5

Colourful confusion

Many insects fool predators by looking like something else or by camouflage colours which match their backgrounds.

Bay-headed Tanager

Which way? ▶

Hairstreak butterflies have a dummy head on their hind wings. On landing, they move their wings up and down. This waggles the false antennae and makes them look real. A bird will probably peck at the false head rather than the real one. The butterfly then escapes with only slightly damaged wings.

Head

This South American hairstreak will fly "the wrong way" to escape, confusing the bird.

False antennae

Another model: a poisonous African Monarch.

The Mocker Swallowtail ▼

Birds quickly learn the colour patterns of poisonous butterflies and leave them alone. Edible butterflies which have the same patterns are protected. Female Mocker Swallowtails have the added advantage of looking like several poisonous species. Males, strangely, never mimic and so are unprotected.

One model: a poisonous Friar butterfly.

Two mimics: both are female Mocker Swallowtails.

Curious caterpillars ▶

Caterpillars make juicy meals but protect themselves from birds by various disguises. Some look like bird droppings, others like twigs, and some match the colours of leaves. The Lobster Moth caterpillar even squirts acid.

This threatening "snake" is actually a hawk moth caterpillar. It waves its body to look like a snake.

Not a twig but a caterpillar holding itself rigid.

The false eyes are on the underside.

Careful disguise ▼

Birds remember being stung and avoid insects that resemble wasps. Yellow and black are warning colours in nature.

The harmless Hornet Moth of Europe and North America mimics the stinging Hornet.

This Hairy Buprestid beetle looks like a wasp even when flying, because it keeps its wing-cases over its back.

A flash of colour

Camouflage gives no protection once a hungry predator has spotted its meal. But a sudden display of bright colours and patterns startles the predator and gives the prey a few seconds in which to escape.

A flightless Australian Mountain Grasshopper shows its bright body.

Flower mantis with butterfly prey.

Dangerous flower ▶

Flower mantids feed on insects and seem to lie in wait on flowers that match their own colours. Some are green to match green petals while others are pink, matching pink petals. Markings and projections on their bodies and legs perfect the camouflage.

Tail "whips" wave menacingly.

A Puss Moth caterpillar, when attacked, spits out its stomach contents and acid from a special gland. Large false eyes form a fierce "face".

TRUE or FALSE?

Zebras have black and white fleas.

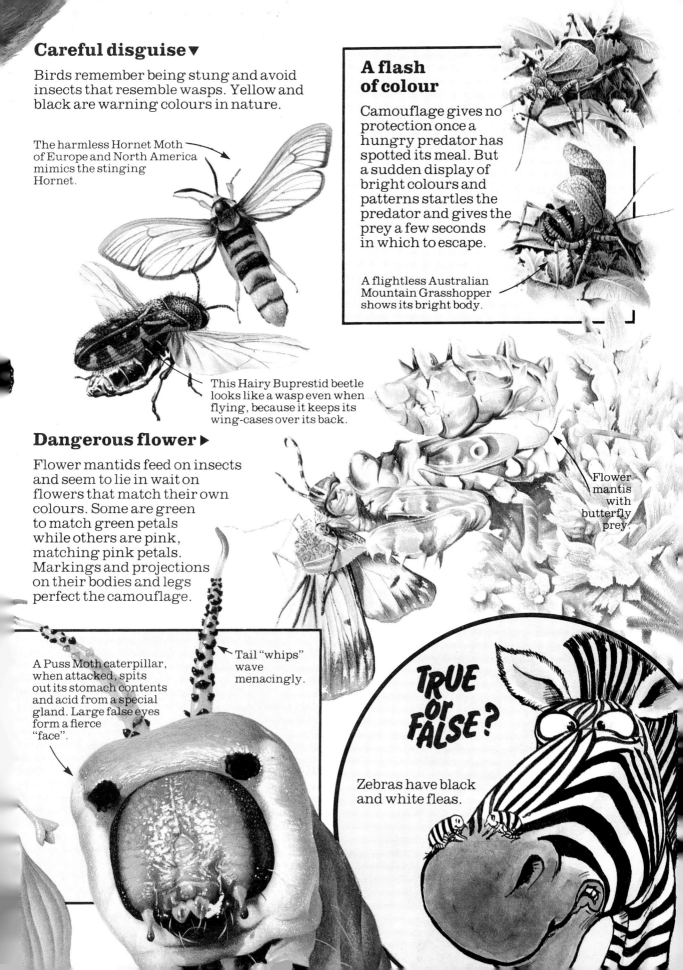

Food and feeding

Insects eat plants or animals, alive or dead, as well as substances produced by them. Some have amazing methods of using unlikely sources of food.

Toad-in-the-hole ▶

The larvae of a horsefly lie buried in mud at the edge of ponds in the U.S.A., ready to grab tiny Spade-foot Toads as they emerge from the water. A larva grasps a toadlet with its mouth hooks and injects a slow-acting poison. Then it drags its meal into the mud and sucks out the juices. It leaves the rest of the body to rot. Adult horseflies, however, are likely to be eaten by adult toads.

Young Spade-foot Toad.

The toadlet and the horsefly larva are each about two centimetres long.

The larva is a grub-like stage between the egg and adult horsefly.

Disappearing dung

Dung beetles bury the dung of grazing mammals and lay their eggs on it. They react to smell, moving towards buffalo dung before it hits the ground. A single mass of fresh elephant dung may hold 7,000 beetles. Within a day or two, they will have buried it all.

Some beetles roll away dung with their back legs.

▼ Turning the tables

A sundew plant feeds on insects which are trapped by sticky droplets on the stalks on its leaves. But caterpillars of a small plume moth feed on sundews in Florida, U.S.A. Detachable scales on the moth probably save it from being caught. The caterpillars drink the sticky droplets, then eat the stalks and any trapped insects.

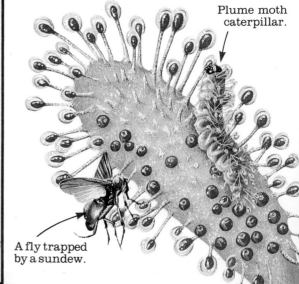

Plume moth caterpillar.

A fly trapped by a sundew.

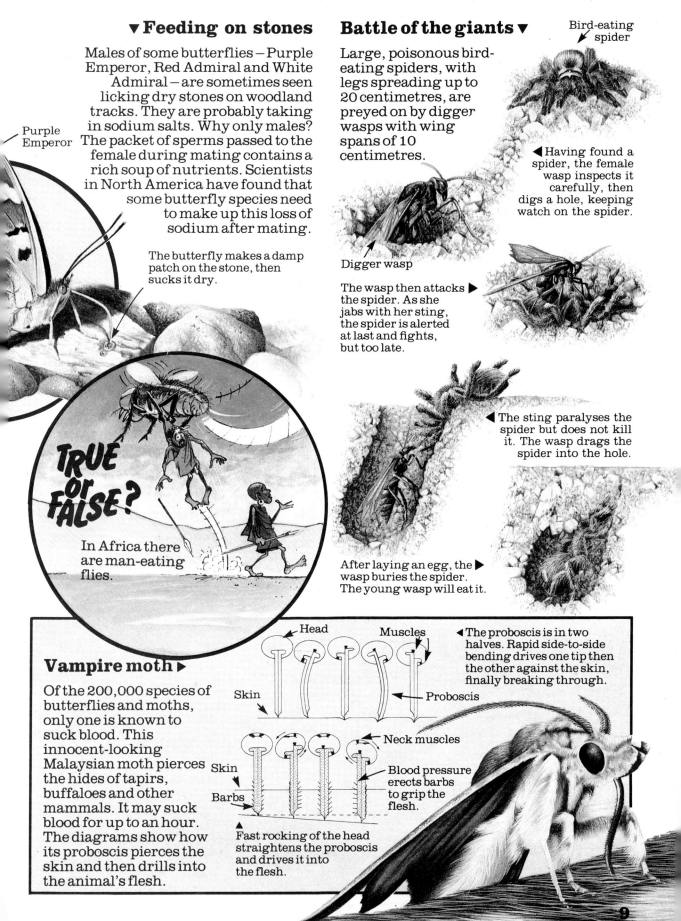

▼ Feeding on stones

Males of some butterflies – Purple Emperor, Red Admiral and White Admiral – are sometimes seen licking dry stones on woodland tracks. They are probably taking in sodium salts. Why only males? The packet of sperms passed to the female during mating contains a rich soup of nutrients. Scientists in North America have found that some butterfly species need to make up this loss of sodium after mating.

Purple Emperor

The butterfly makes a damp patch on the stone, then sucks it dry.

Battle of the giants ▼

Large, poisonous bird-eating spiders, with legs spreading up to 20 centimetres, are preyed on by digger wasps with wing spans of 10 centimetres.

Bird-eating spider

Digger wasp

◀ Having found a spider, the female wasp inspects it carefully, then digs a hole, keeping watch on the spider.

The wasp then attacks ▶ the spider. As she jabs with her sting, the spider is alerted at last and fights, but too late.

◀ The sting paralyses the spider but does not kill it. The wasp drags the spider into the hole.

After laying an egg, the ▶ wasp buries the spider. The young wasp will eat it.

TRUE or FALSE?

In Africa there are man-eating flies.

Vampire moth ▶

Of the 200,000 species of butterflies and moths, only one is known to suck blood. This innocent-looking Malaysian moth pierces the hides of tapirs, buffaloes and other mammals. It may suck blood for up to an hour. The diagrams show how its proboscis pierces the skin and then drills into the animal's flesh.

Head

Muscles

Skin

Proboscis

◀ The proboscis is in two halves. Rapid side-to-side bending drives one tip then the other against the skin, finally breaking through.

Skin

Neck muscles

Barbs

Blood pressure erects barbs to grip the flesh.

▲ Fast rocking of the head straightens the proboscis and drives it into the flesh.

Chemical warfare

Harmful chemicals are used by insects as repellents, in defence and attack. Most advertise this by their colour pattern, often some combination of black with yellow, orange or red. These colours are a universal code meaning "don't touch!"

Frothing at the mouth ▶

Flightless Lubber Grasshoppers are large and slow. When disturbed, however, they ooze foul-smelling froth from the mouth and thorax with a hissing noise. Air is bubbled into a mixture of chemicals which include phenol and quinones. Both these chemicals are widely used as repellents by insects.

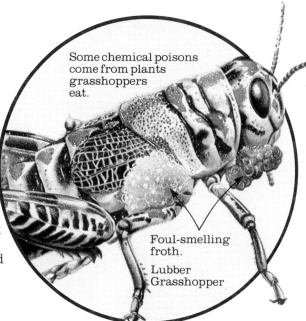

Some chemical poisons come from plants grasshoppers eat.

Foul-smelling froth.

Lubber Grasshopper

◀ Painful jabs

The stings of ants, bees and wasps are modified ovipositors (egg-laying tools), used to inject poison in defence or to paralyse prey. More than 50 different chemicals have been identified from various species. Some cause itching, pain, swelling and redness; others destroy cells and spread the poison. Honeybees cannot pull their barbed stings from human skins, and tear themselves away, dying soon afterwards.

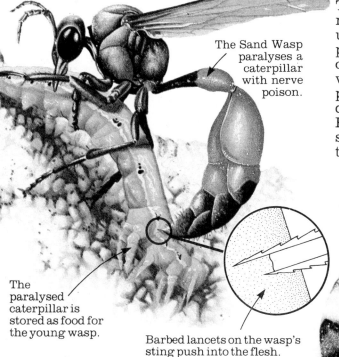

The Sand Wasp paralyses a caterpillar with nerve poison.

The paralysed caterpillar is stored as food for the young wasp.

Barbed lancets on the wasp's sting push into the flesh.

Bombardment ▶

When provoked, a bombardier beetle swivels the tip of its abdomen and shoots a jet of boiling chemicals at its attacker. The chemicals are produced in a "reaction chamber" with an explosion you can hear. The spray of foul-tasting, burning vapour is a result of rapid firing. It shoots out at 500 to 1,000 pulses per second at a temperature of 100°C.

Bottoms up ▶

Darkling beetles respond to trouble by doing a hand-stand. They tilt up at an angle of 45° and point their abdomen at the attacker. They then spray a foul-smelling liquid from glands that open at the tip of the abdomen. Darkling beetles are slower than bombardier beetles and are often swallowed by toads before discharging their spray.

The foul spray contains quinone.

Darkling beetle

A Grasshopper Mouse disarms a beetle by ramming its hind end into the soil. It eats all but the poison.

Multi-purpose hairs

The hairs of Yellow-tail Moth caterpillars can cause a nasty rash. Adult females keep a tuft of these irritant hairs and shed them over their eggs for protection.

Food as a weapon ▶

Sawfly larvae that feed on pine needles, store the scented resins in pouches which open into the gut just behind the head. Under attack, a larva vomits a sticky blob of resin, twists itself round, and daubs the attacker, gumming its legs together.

A sawfly larva gumming up an ant.

The bombardier beetle's spray can be fired accurately in any direction.

Ladybirds bite when annoyed.

TRUE or FALSE?

Curious courtship

Insects have many ways of attracting and recognising a mate, of arousing their interest, calming their fears, and overcoming their aggression.

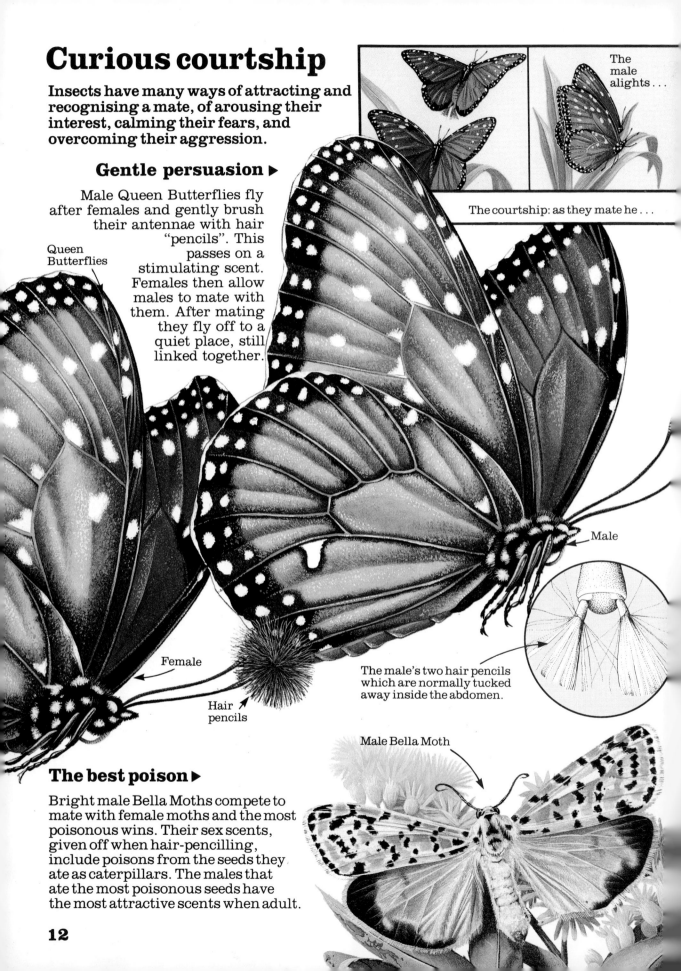

The male alights . . .

The courtship: as they mate he . . .

Gentle persuasion ▶

Male Queen Butterflies fly after females and gently brush their antennae with hair "pencils". This passes on a stimulating scent. Females then allow males to mate with them. After mating they fly off to a quiet place, still linked together.

Queen Butterflies

Female

Hair pencils

Male

The male's two hair pencils which are normally tucked away inside the abdomen.

Male Bella Moth

The best poison ▶

Bright male Bella Moths compete to mate with female moths and the most poisonous wins. Their sex scents, given off when hair-pencilling, include poisons from the seeds they ate as caterpillars. The males that ate the most poisonous seeds have the most attractive scents when adult.

. . . they mate . . .

. . . and fly off together.

. . . strokes her antennae as if to calm her.

TRUE or FALSE?

Singing crickets attract more females.

Off with his head!

In some species of preying mantis, the female begins to eat the male while they are mating. She starts at his head and by the time she reaches his abdomen, mating is completed. By becoming a nourishing meal, the father provides a supply of food for the eggs that are his children.

Bribing the lady ▼

Courtship and mating are dangerous for males if females are insect-eaters. Many male Empid flies distract their females with the gift of a captured insect. This stops the female eating the male. Some wrap the "gift" in silk.

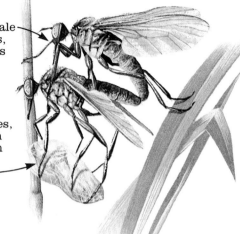

While the female Empid fly eats, the male mates with her.

In nectar-feeding species, males offer an empty balloon of silk – a ritual gift.

Fatal attraction ▼

Male and female fireflies recognise and find each other by light signals. Each species has its own pattern of flashes. Predatory female *Photuris* mimic the signals of female *Photinus* to lure male *Photinus* to their deaths. As their male prey approaches, they take off and "home in" like light-seeking missiles.

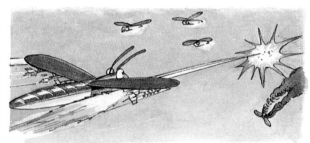

Female firefly

A female flashing in answer to a male.

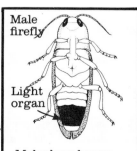

Male firefly

Light organ

Males have larger lights than females.

Magical changes

Grasshoppers and several other sorts of insects hatch out of eggs as miniature adults, except for their wings and reproductive organs which develop later.▶

In many other groups of insects, such as beetles and flies, the young insect (the larva) is quite unlike the adult. The larva concentrates on feeding and growing before turning into a pupa. Great changes of the body take place in the pupa to produce the winged adult.▼

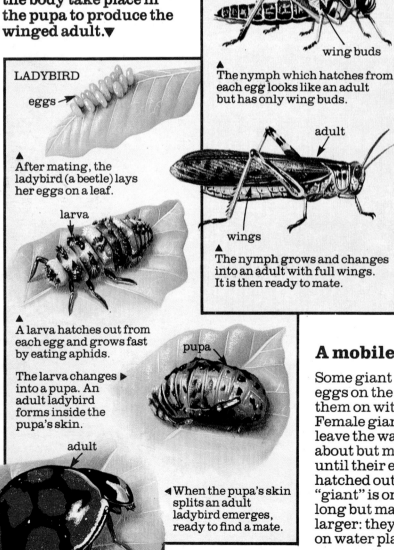

LOCUST

▲ A locust lays her eggs in damp, warm soil and leaves them to hatch.

nymph

wing buds

▲ The nymph which hatches from each egg looks like an adult but has only wing buds.

adult

wings

▲ The nymph grows and changes into an adult with full wings. It is then ready to mate.

LADYBIRD

eggs

▲ After mating, the ladybird (a beetle) lays her eggs on a leaf.

larva

▲ A larva hatches out from each egg and grows fast by eating aphids.

The larva changes ▶ into a pupa. An adult ladybird forms inside the pupa's skin.

pupa

adult

◀ When the pupa's skin splits an adult ladybird emerges, ready to find a mate.

▼ Egg machines

Moth caterpillars, known as bag-worms, build a protective case of silk and fragments of twigs and leaves. They pupate in the case, and the wingless females never leave. Many females are worm-like, with no legs, eyes or mouthparts. Their only function is to mate and lay eggs. Males are normal. Three of the many different bag-worms are shown here.

A North American bag-worm caterpillar eating leaves.

A case becomes a cocoon.

A male Malayan bag-worm mating. The female is still inside her case.

A mobile nest ▶

Some giant water bugs lay their eggs on the male's back, sticking them on with waterproof "glue". Female giant water bugs often leave the water and fly about but males stay until their eggs have hatched out. This "giant" is only 2-5 cm long but many are larger: they lay eggs on water plants.

The male "nursemaid".

Beauty and the beast ▶

The nymphs of dragonflies are fearsome underwater predators, even eating small fish. By pumping water in and out of its rectum, where its gills are, a nymph can move by jet propulsion.

A fully-grown nymph climbs out of the water and a dragonfly emerges.

Adult dragonfly

A nymph eating a tadpole, caught by hooks on its lower lip.

Coming out together

The periodical cicadas of the eastern United States spend 17 years (13 in the south) below ground as nymphs feeding on tree roots. All in one place emerge together. They change into adults, lay eggs, and after a few weeks die. None is seen again for 17 (or 13) years.

TRUE or FALSE?

Butterflies live for only one day.

A red aphid giving birth. Other daughters cluster behind her.

Nymphs hatch from the eggs.

Inside a Russian doll is a smaller doll and within that is a still smaller doll, and so on . . .

Giant water bug

Russian dolls ▲

For most of the year, female aphids produce young without mating. Eggs develop into small daughters inside the mother. Inside each daughter eggs also start to develop. So when a mother gives birth to her daughters, they already contain her grand-daughters, like a set of dolls.

Royal households

The social life of two different groups of insects: ants, bees and wasps, and termites, has evolved separately. Most nests have only one egg-laying female, known as the queen. The teeming members of a nest are her offspring. Most are workers who never breed. The queen keeps her ruling position and controls the nests' activities by chemical communication.

The queen honeybee is at the centre of the swarm.

Deciding where to go ▶

A new honeybee nest starts when thousands of workers, all female, leave the old nest with the old queen, or with some virgin queens, when a few males (drones) go too. Before they fly off, scout bees find suitable nesting sites and report back, telling of their finds by "dancing". After several hours, by unknown means, the site for the new nest is chosen.

Bees swarm on the ground, on branches and even on post-boxes in towns.

To fill her crop with nectar, a bee worker visits up to 1,000 flowers. She flies 10 such trips a day if it is sunny.

To make 1 kg of honey, bees make up to 65,000 trips, visiting 45-64 million flowers.

Large colonies have 80,000 workers and eat 225 kg of honey a year. Surplus honey is stored for bad weather.

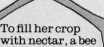

Honeycomb cells are six-sided.

TRUE or FALSE?

Bees make jellies.

Incredible industry ▶

Vespula wasps build their football-sized nests with paper made of chewed-up wood mixed with saliva. A large nest has 12 combs containing 15,000 cells, surrounded by walls of layered paper. Unlike the honeybees, wasps abandon their nests in autumn and build a new one in spring, sometimes underground in an old animal burrow.

Dominant *Polistes* worker biting a subordinate.

Bullying ends in food exchange.

Nest bullies ▲

Dominant *Polistes* wasp workers bully their sister workers. A dominant one will bite a subordinate, as she crouches motionless, until she regurgitates her food. This seems to bind the colony together.

Wasps do not make honey but feed their larvae on pellets made of chewed-up insects.

◀ Equipped for the job

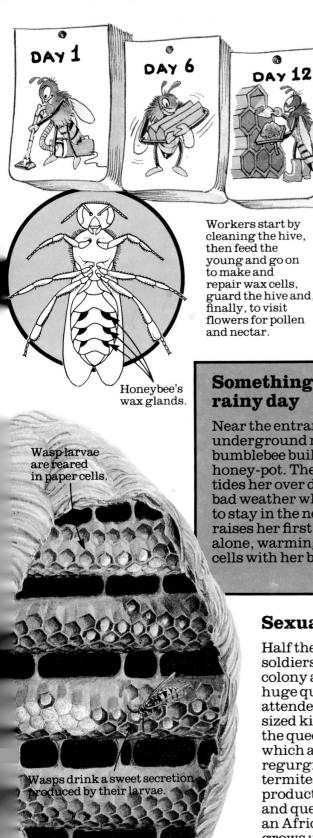

DAY 1

DAY 6

DAY 12

DAY 19

DAY 26

As a worker honeybee grows older, her body changes for different tasks. Her salivary glands start to produce "brood food" for the larvae on the fifth or sixth day. This stops by the twelfth day and glands on her abdomen start to produce wax. Such tasks largely depend on a bee's age although the time-table is not rigid. Workers live for 6-8 weeks. Queens can live for up to 5 years.

Workers start by cleaning the hive, then feed the young and go on to make and repair wax cells, guard the hive and, finally, to visit flowers for pollen and nectar.

Honeybee's wax glands.

Wasp larvae are reared in paper cells.

Wasps drink a sweet secretion produced by their larvae.

Something for a rainy day

Near the entrance to her underground nest, a queen bumblebee builds a wax honey-pot. The stored food tides her over days of bad weather when she has to stay in the nest. She raises her first brood alone, warming the egg cells with her body heat.

A queen bumblebee may nest in an old mouse nest.

Queen bumblebee

Honey-pot

Cocoons of the first brood.

Sexual equality ▶

Half the workers and soldiers in a termite colony are male and the huge queen is constantly attended by a normal-sized king. Chemicals in the queen's droppings, which are eaten and regurgitated by the termites, prevent the production of more kings and queens. The queen of an African termite species grows up to 140 mm long and can lay 30,000 eggs a day. Queens may live for 15 years and more.

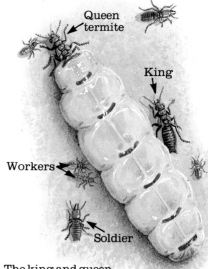

Queen termite

King

Workers

Soldier

The king and queen never leave the royal chamber.

Farmers, tailors, soldiers and builders

Large insect colonies, particularly those of termites and ants, have different members which are specialized for different types of jobs. By working together efficiently, they have developed unusual ways of using and feeding on plants and other animals.

The abdomen may be 1 cm in diameter.

Honey-pot ant

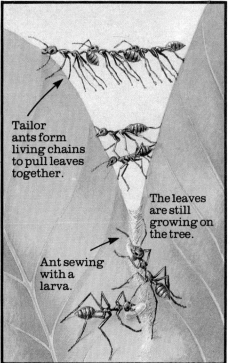

Tailor ants form living chains to pull leaves together.

The leaves are still growing on the tree.

Ant sewing with a larva.

◄ Tailor ants

Oecophylla ants sew leaves together to form a nest, using silk produced by the saliva glands of their larvae. A line of workers stand on the edge of one leaf, and pull another towards it with their jaws. Other workers wave larvae to and fro across the leaves until they are joined by the silk. Tailor ants live in the forests of Africa, S.E. Asia and Australia.

Minders ►

When cutting or carrying bits of leaf, leaf-cutter ants cannot defend themselves against parasitic flies. Tiny workers, too small to cut and carry leaves, go with the larger workers to fight off the flies. The ants carry the leaf pieces back to their nest.

Once in the nest the leaves are chewed up, mixed with saliva and droppings, and used as a compost for the fungus which the ants feed on.

Parasitic fly

A small worker acts as bodyguard.

Leaf-cutter ants can strip a fruit tree bare overnight.

A section cut through a termite mound, showing the queen's chamber, air-conditioning channels and fungus gardens.

Channels control climate and air flow.

Royal chamber

Fungus gardens

The fungus gardens break down plant material. Termites feed on the white blobs.

A worker feeding.

Honey-pot ants are a sweet delicacy to Mexican villagers and Australian aborigines. An ant colony may have up to 300 living "honey-pots".

Living storage tanks ▲

Some honey-pot ant workers are fed so much nectar and honeydew that their abdomens swell to the size of a grape. Unable to move, they hang motionless from the roof of the nest and are looked after by other workers. The "honey-pots" store food for the colony to eat when the nectar season is over in the deserts where they live. When empty they shrivel up.

Soldiers and weapons

Soldier termites have enlarged heads and defend the nest against intruders. Most have formidable pointed jaws as weapons, but not *Nasutitermes* soldiers. Their heads extend forwards as a pointed nozzle from which they spray a sticky, irritating fluid.

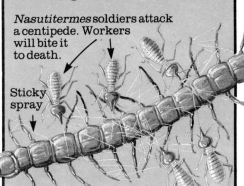

Nasutitermes soldiers attack a centipede. Workers will bite it to death.

Sticky spray

Master builders

Fungus garden termites build enormous, rock-hard mounds with sand, clay and saliva. One vast mound contained 11,750 tonnes of sand, piled up grain by grain. The nest may be in or below the mound and the shape varies with species, soil type and rainfall. Some mounds are 9 m tall.

Some mounds are like pagodas, with roofs to shed rain.

Mounds of the Australian Compass Termite all face the same way. The broad sides, facing east-west, catch maximum heat from the weak sun at dawn and dusk.

5 m

▼ Laying in a store

Harvester termites cut grass into short pieces and store it in their warm, damp underground nests where temperatures are constant. Harvester ants bring seeds from the desert floor into their underground granaries. Husked and chewed into "ant bread", it provides food during shortages.

Fresh grass is stored in chambers near the surface. When dry it is then moved close to the nest.

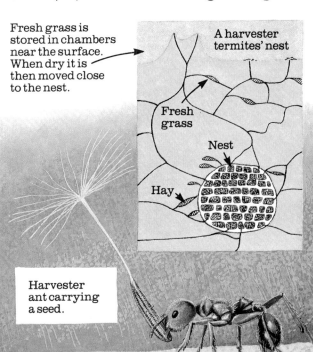

A harvester termites' nest

Fresh grass

Nest

Hay

Harvester ant carrying a seed.

Recognition and deception

Scent, sight and sound are used by insects to identify each other and to pass on information to members of the same species. They may also be used for defence and disguise.

A colony of aphids.

Lacewing larva covered with aphid wax.

Tiger moth

Flexing this cuticle makes a clicking noise.

The ear picks up a bat's clicks.

Bright colours deter daytime predators.

Wolf in sheep's clothing

Woolly Alder Aphids are eaten by Green Lacewing larvae in disguise, despite being protected by ants that feed on their honeydew. The larvae pluck wax from the aphids, and attach it to hooks on their backs.

If stripped of its wax, a lacewing larva is removed by an ant.

Noises in the night

Many nasty-tasting tiger moths make high-pitched clicks at night. Bats, which hunt by echo-location, veer away from clicking moths. The Banded Woolly Bear Moth is quite edible but it clicks like other tiger moths and so is left alone by the bats.

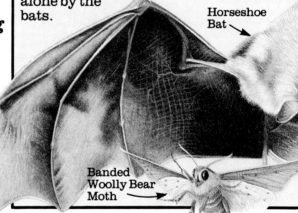

Horseshoe Bat

Banded Woolly Bear Moth

Turning up the volume

Mole crickets broadcast their songs from specially built burrows. The Y-shaped burrow acts as an amplifier so that the call can be heard from further away.

Noses on stalks ▶

An insect's antennae carry dozens of tiny structures which are sensitive to scent. They are also sensitive to touch. Antennae are used both to smell and to touch and stroke. They provide an insect with much information.

Cockchafers spread their antennae to find food.

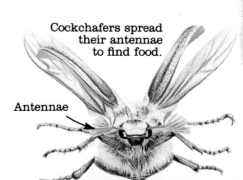

Antennae

Emperor Moth

20

Grasshopper band ▶

Male grasshoppers stridulate, or sing, by rubbing a "file" across a "scraper". They mainly sing to attract female grasshoppers.

A line of pegs on the inside of the "thigh" acts as the file. They rub across a hard vein on the wing.

"Ear"

Close-up of pegs.

Short-horned grasshoppers rub the hind legs against the wings. Their "ears" are on the side of the body.

Scraper

File

A scraper on one wing rubs against a file on the other.

"Ears" are in their front "knees".

Long-horned grasshoppers rub their wings together. Their "ears" are in their front "knees".

TRUE or FALSE?

Crickets have thermometers.

The large feathery antennae of the male Emperor Moth can detect a female's scent from several miles.

No one is sure why these antennae are so long.

Timberman Beetle

Dancing bees ▼

Honeybees tell others where to find food by "dancing" on the comb. Sound, scent and food-sharing also pass on information about the type of food and where it is.

Round dance
A round dance means food within 80 m. The richness of the source is shown by the energy and length of dance. Other bees pick up the scent of the flowers.

Honeybees

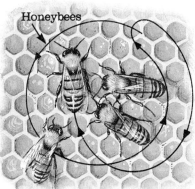

Waggle dance

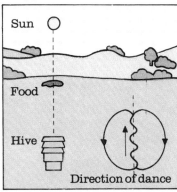

Sun

Food

Hive

Direction of dance

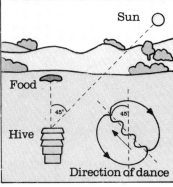

Sun

Food

45°

Hive

45°

Direction of dance

A waggle dance describes food over 80 m from the hive. Speed and number of waggles on the straight run indicate distance. The angle between

straight run and vertical shows the direction of the food relative to the sun. As the sun moves across the sky, the angle of dance changes.

Living – and dying – together

Many insects live with and make use of a wide variety of other animals and plants. Some even share ants' nests and many are "milked" of sweet liquids by ants. These relationships have led to special ways of feeding, finding shelter and breeding. Sometimes the association is good for both sides. More often, one makes use of the other, usually by eating it.

Over 100 moths, of seven species, have been found in the coat of one sloth.

Three-toed Sloth

Special delivery ▼

Human Botflies use biting flies, such as mosquitoes, to deliver their eggs to human, bird or mammal hosts. Grubs hatch from the eggs and burrow into the host's skin.

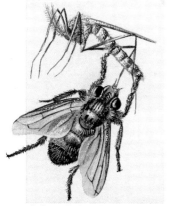

A female botfly catches a mosquito and glues a cluster of 15-20 eggs on the mosquito's body.

When the mosquito settles on a person, the eggs hatch immediately in response to warmth.

Moths and sloths ▲

Sloths are so sluggish that moths infest their long coats which are green with algae. About once a week, a sloth slowly descends its tree to excrete. Its moths lay eggs in the dung, which the caterpillars eat. Since their "home" never moves far or fast, moths have no trouble finding it again.

Velvet ant

Solitary wasp pupa.

◄ Pretty but painful

Velvet ants are not ants. They are really densely hairy, wingless, female wasps. Most break into the nests of solitary bees or wasps to lay their eggs on a pupa, which the velvet ant grub will eat. The brilliant colours of the wasps perhaps warn that they have a sting so powerful they are called "cow-killers".

A houseful of lodgers ▶

Robin's pincushions on wild rose are galls caused by a tiny wasp which lays eggs in young leaf buds. After the gall has formed, another gall wasp enters and lays its eggs. The larvae of both owner and lodger are parasitized by chalcid and ichneumon wasps, and these in turn may also be parasitized.

The original Robin's pincushion gall wasp.

Gall wasp larvae inside the pincushion.

TRUE or FALSE?

Springtail "jockeys" ride soldier termites.

Treacherous guest ▼

Although they eat ant larvae, caterpillars of the Large Blue Butterfly are allowed to live in the nests of *Myrmica* ants. They produce a sweet fluid which the ants love.

Tiny caterpillars eat Thyme flowers. Older ones will produce a sweet fluid for an ant, which responds by carrying it into its nest.

Caterpillar in ant nest.

Ants' nest.

Adult Large Blue

Parasites on parasites

The Mexican Bean Beetle eats leaves and is a pest in North America. It is parasitized by a tachinid fly, which is itself parasitized by an ichneumon wasp.

Mexican Bean Beetle

Tachinid fly

Ichneumon wasp

Beetle's larva

Wasp laying eggs in the fly's pupa

Fly larva inside beetle larva

Travellers and hitchhikers

Insects not only make long journeys under their own power but are also carried, often accidentally, by people or other animals.

Giant Wood-wasp

Ovipositor

Long-distance travel

Most Monarch butterflies of eastern North America spend the winter in mountain conifer forests in Mexico. Only one roost is known, although there are thought to be others. More than 14 million Monarchs cluster on trunks and branches of an area only about 125 metres across. Surprisingly, the roost was not found until 1975.

U.S.A.

Mexico

The map shows where Monarchs spend the summer (pink area) and winter (blue area). The arrows show the routes of their migration flights. The two-way flight, south and then north to the breeding areas, averages 4,000 kilometres.

← Monarchs settle to roost when the temperature falls below 15°C.

Monarch

▲ Surprise visitor

Female Giant Wood-wasps, or Horntails, use their long ovipositors to lay eggs deep in felled or dying conifers. The larvae take up to 3 years to develop, by which time the timber may have been used for building. Adults can emerge far from their forest.

Gatecrasher ▶

An African moth previously unknown in Britain was caught one July night in Buckingham Palace gardens. Its caterpillars eat the flower buds of cotton and cocoa. Could it have been unwittingly imported, as pupa or adult, in the clothes of a garden party guest?

A swarm of Desert Locusts.

The greatest recorded swarm of locusts covered 5,180 km².

Drifts of butterflies ▶

White butterflies in the drier parts of Africa fly off in huge clouds at the start of the dry season when there is no food for the caterpillars. One observer in East Africa reported 500 million butterflies passing each day on a 24 kilometre wide front. Migrating butterflies are sometimes blown out to sea and then washed up on beaches.

TRUE or FALSE? Young beetles hitch lifts on bees.

Far from water

Large numbers of *Sympetrum* dragonflies fly south in autumn across France and through mountain passes in the Pyrenees. The exact route of their migration is not known but some turn up in Portugal. On northward migrations the dragonflies often reach south-eastern England from Europe.

Migrating dragonflies

▼ Locust plagues

From time to time Desert Locusts breed rapidly and millions fly long distances in search of food. An area of 26 million km², from West Africa to Assam, and Turkey to Tanzania is at risk of invasion. A large swarm eats 80,000 tonnes of grain and vegetation a day.

Mulberry Silkworm Moth

The caterpillar is called a silkworm.

Caterpillars are fed on mulberry leaves, and pupate in a cocoon spun from a single thread of silk over 900 m long.

Cocoon

Home-grown moths ▲

Silkworm Moths have been reared in China for their silk for over 4,000 years. The moth's wings are so small it cannot fly and it no longer exists in the wild.

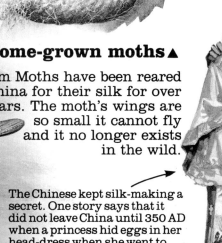

The Chinese kept silk-making a secret. One story says that it did not leave China until 350 AD when a princess hid eggs in her head-dress when she went to India to marry a prince.

Citizens of the world

Wherever you go on land you find insects.
They can live in the harshest climates, eat
whatever there is, and adapt quickly to change.

TRUE or FALSE?

Insects make long-distance 'phone calls.

Drinking fog ▶

Darkling beetles manage to
live in the hottest, most
barren parts of the Namib
desert. When night-time
fogs roll in from the sea,
Onymacris beetles climb to
the top of sand dunes and,
head down, stand facing
into the wind. Moisture
condenses on ridges on
their backs and runs down
into their mouths.

Staying on top of the world ▶

Above 5,000 metres on
Kilimanjaro, just below
the snow cap, is a bleak,
windy, alpine desert, with
little vegetation. Moths,
beetles, earwigs, crane
flies and grasshoppers
live there but many are
wingless. Flying insects
might be in danger
of blowing away.

Mount Kilimanjaro

A flightless crane fly

Hot as your bath ▶

In the USA's Yellowstone
National Park, famous for
its geysers, nymphs of
the Green-jacket Skimmer
dragonfly live in hot
spring water at 40°C.

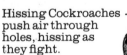

Hissing Cockroaches
push air through
holes, hissing as
they fight.

Cockroaches nibble at book-bindings,
photographic film, starched
linen, leather goods and
any food, fouling them
with strong-smelling
droppings.

Easy to please

Tropical cockroaches have spread
worldwide as scavengers in
people's heated houses. They can
and do eat anything of animal or
plant origin, and this
accounts for
their success.

This cave cockroach from
Trinidad feeds on bat
droppings.

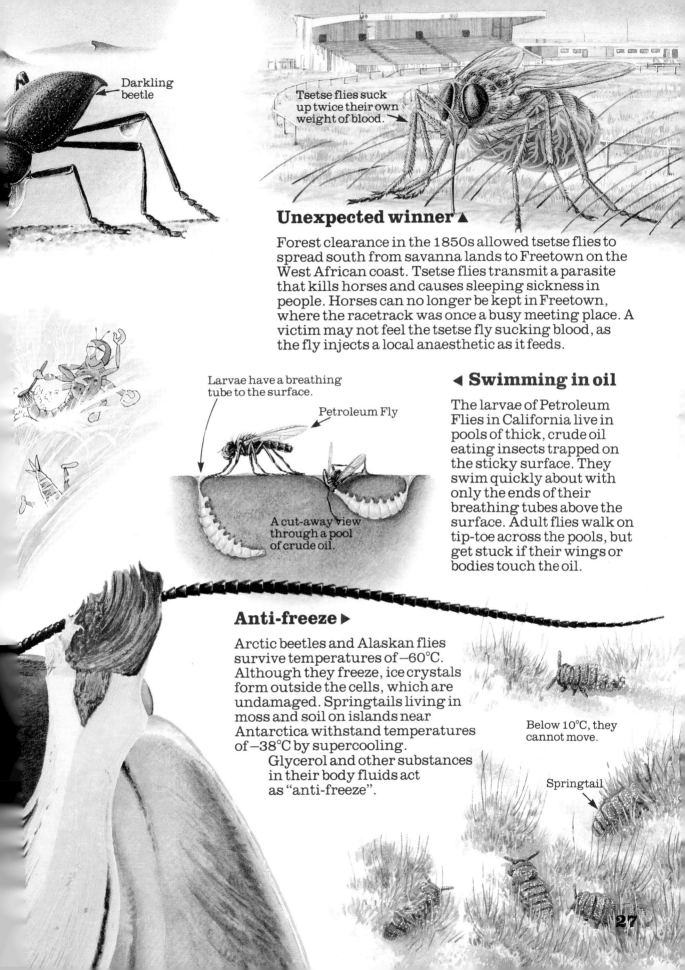

Darkling beetle

Tsetse flies suck up twice their own weight of blood.

Unexpected winner ▲

Forest clearance in the 1850s allowed tsetse flies to spread south from savanna lands to Freetown on the West African coast. Tsetse flies transmit a parasite that kills horses and causes sleeping sickness in people. Horses can no longer be kept in Freetown, where the racetrack was once a busy meeting place. A victim may not feel the tsetse fly sucking blood, as the fly injects a local anaesthetic as it feeds.

Larvae have a breathing tube to the surface.

Petroleum Fly

A cut-away view through a pool of crude oil.

◄ Swimming in oil

The larvae of Petroleum Flies in California live in pools of thick, crude oil eating insects trapped on the sticky surface. They swim quickly about with only the ends of their breathing tubes above the surface. Adult flies walk on tip-toe across the pools, but get stuck if their wings or bodies touch the oil.

Anti-freeze ▶

Arctic beetles and Alaskan flies survive temperatures of −60°C. Although they freeze, ice crystals form outside the cells, which are undamaged. Springtails living in moss and soil on islands near Antarctica withstand temperatures of −38°C by supercooling. Glycerol and other substances in their body fluids act as "anti-freeze".

Below 10°C, they cannot move.

Springtail

Insect mysteries

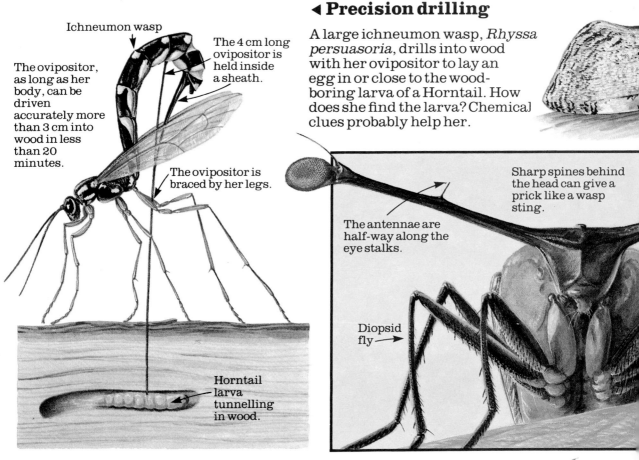

Ichneumon wasp

The ovipositor, as long as her body, can be driven accurately more than 3 cm into wood in less than 20 minutes.

The 4 cm long ovipositor is held inside a sheath.

The ovipositor is braced by her legs.

Horntail larva tunnelling in wood.

◄ Precision drilling

A large ichneumon wasp, *Rhyssa persuasoria*, drills into wood with her ovipositor to lay an egg in or close to the wood-boring larva of a Horntail. How does she find the larva? Chemical clues probably help her.

The antennae are half-way along the eye stalks.

Sharp spines behind the head can give a prick like a wasp sting.

Diopsid fly

Samson's riddle ▼

In the story of Samson, in The Bible, Samson found a swarm of bees and honey in the body of a lion he had earlier killed. Could the bees have been drone flies – a type of hoverfly which mimics honeybees? Drone flies, unlike bees, sometimes breed in rotting carcasses.

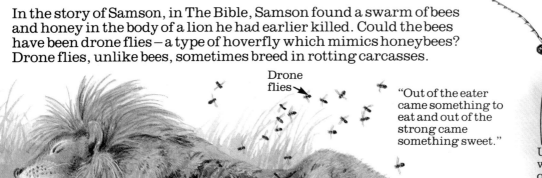

Drone flies

"Out of the eater came something to eat and out of the strong came something sweet."

Unlike most weevils, this one has a short snout.

This weevil's scientific name is *Tribus attelabini*.

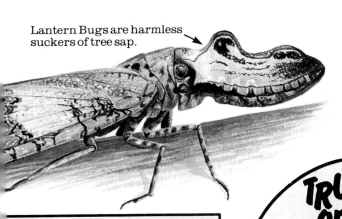

Lantern Bugs are harmless suckers of tree sap.

◀ Miniature monsters

The huge heads of Lantern Bugs were once thought to be luminous which is how they got their name. Why do they look so odd? Could a monkey mistake this 10 cm long bug for an alligator?

TRUE or FALSE?

Maggots help doctors.

Green Metallic Beetle from Malaysia.

Stalked eyes

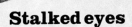

Why should the eyes of diopsid flies be on long stalks? One suggestion is that diopsids mimic wasps. Their stalked eyes look like wasps' antennae. They are common in damp, shady places, crawling around on top of leaves and behaving more like small wasps than flies.

A North American metallic wood-boring beetle.

Precious beetles

Amongst the most brilliantly coloured insects are metallic wood-boring beetles but the purpose of their colour is unclear. Their shining wing-cases have been used in jewellery and embroidery. Some people have even worn tethered beetles as brooches. Toasted larvae of the Green Metallic Beetle are a delicacy.

▼ Insect "giraffe"

This odd weevil from the island of Madagascar, off Africa, has a very long head, rather than a long, giraffe-like neck. No one is quite sure why it is this shape. When threatened, it drops down and plays dead. (It is closely related to the red weevil on the front cover.)

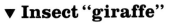

It is 2.5 cm long and the head takes up almost half this length.

Warning mimicry? ▶

On hearing a foot-step, worker termites foraging beneath dead leaves, vibrate their abdomens. When there are many of them, the rustling of leaves sounds like the hiss of a snake.

SSSSSSS

Record breakers

Largest and smallest butterflies

Queen Alexandra's Birdwing from New Guinea has a wingspan of 28 cm; that of a blue butterfly from Africa is only 1.4 cm.

Loudest insect

Male cicadas produce the loudest insect sound, by vibrating ribbed plates in a pair of amplifying cavities at the base of the abdomen: this can be heard over 400 m away.

Population explosion

If all the offspring of a pair of fruit flies survived and bred, the 25th generation — one year later — would form a ball of flies that would reach nearly from the earth to the sun.

Fastest flight

The record has been claimed for a hawk moth flying at 53.6 km/h, but it probably had a following wind. A more reliable record is 28.57 km/h for a dragonfly *Anax parthenope*.

Killer bees

So-called killer bees are an African strain of honeybee, which tend to attack people and other animals. More than 70 deaths occurred in Venezuela recently in 3 years, the number of stings varying from 200 to over 2,000. In 1964, a Rhodesian survived 2,243 stings.

Fastest runner

Try to catch a cockroach and it seems very elusive. They are among the fastest runners, reaching 30 cm per second, but this is only 1.8 km/h.

Biggest group

The insect order Coleoptera (beetles) includes nearly 330,000 species, about a third of known insects. Roughly 40,000 are weevils.

Shortest life

An aphid may develop in 6 days and live another 4-5 days as an adult. Mayflies have the shortest adult life, many living only one day after emerging from the water.

Oldest group

The oldest fossils of winged insects, dating from more than 300 million years ago, include cockroach wings.

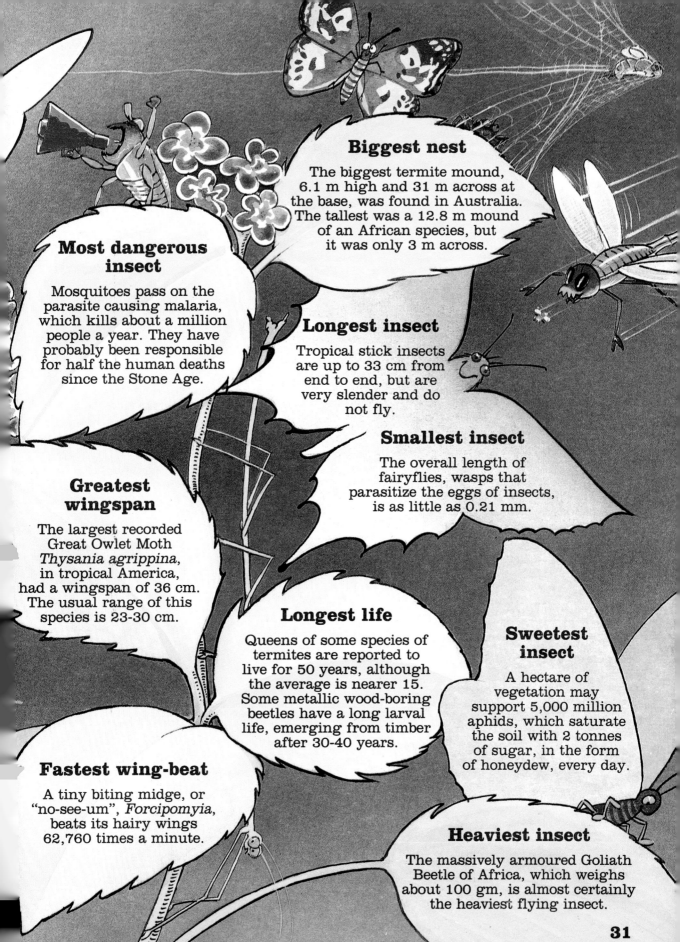

Biggest nest

The biggest termite mound, 6.1 m high and 31 m across at the base, was found in Australia. The tallest was a 12.8 m mound of an African species, but it was only 3 m across.

Most dangerous insect

Mosquitoes pass on the parasite causing malaria, which kills about a million people a year. They have probably been responsible for half the human deaths since the Stone Age.

Longest insect

Tropical stick insects are up to 33 cm from end to end, but are very slender and do not fly.

Smallest insect

The overall length of fairyflies, wasps that parasitize the eggs of insects, is as little as 0.21 mm.

Greatest wingspan

The largest recorded Great Owlet Moth *Thysania agrippina*, in tropical America, had a wingspan of 36 cm. The usual range of this species is 23-30 cm.

Longest life

Queens of some species of termites are reported to live for 50 years, although the average is nearer 15. Some metallic wood-boring beetles have a long larval life, emerging from timber after 30-40 years.

Sweetest insect

A hectare of vegetation may support 5,000 million aphids, which saturate the soil with 2 tonnes of sugar, in the form of honeydew, every day.

Fastest wing-beat

A tiny biting midge, or "no-see-um", *Forcipomyia*, beats its hairy wings 62,760 times a minute.

Heaviest insect

The massively armoured Goliath Beetle of Africa, which weighs about 100 gm, is almost certainly the heaviest flying insect.

Were they true or false?

page 5 Bumblebees have central heating.
TRUE. Bumblebees can maintain a temperature of 30-37°C when the air is near freezing. Heat is produced by a chemical process in the flight muscles.

page 7 Zebras have black and white fleas.
FALSE. A Zebra's fleas are not camouflaged.

page 9 In Africa there are man-eating flies.
TRUE. Maggots of the "tumbu" fly burrow into human skin causing painful open sores.

page 11 Ladybirds bite when annoyed.
FALSE. Blood oozes from their knee joints when they are molested, and this irritates sensitive skins.

page 13 Singing crickets attract more females.
TRUE. Males of a North American cricket attract females by "singing" in groups. Some males never sing but join the group and try to mate.

page 15 Butterflies live for only one day.
FALSE. Some live many months, hibernating in winter, or migrating long distances.

page 16 Bees make jellies.
PARTLY TRUE. The "brood food" produced by worker honeybees is called "royal jelly" because it is given only to future queens.

page 21 Crickets have thermometers.
PARTLY TRUE. The warmer it is, the faster they function. Add 40 to the number of chirps a Snowy Tree Cricket gives in 15 seconds, and you get the temperature in degrees Fahrenheit.

page 23 Springtail "jockeys" ride soldier termites.
TRUE. A West African springtail rides on a soldier's head and snatches its food.

page 25 Young beetles hitch lifts on bees.
TRUE. The larvae of some oil and blister beetles swarm over flowers and attach themselves to bees. Carried to a solitary bee's nest, they invade a brood cell and eat the egg and stored food.

page 26 Insects make long-distance 'phone calls.
FALSE. However, termites frequently bore into underground telephone cables; moisture seeps in, insulation breaks down, and the cable no longer carries messages.

page 29 Maggots help doctors.
PARTLY TRUE. As a result of experience gained in the 1914-18 war, surgeons used maggots of Green-bottle Flies, reared in sterile conditions, to clean infected wounds.

Further reading

The Oxford Book of Insects, J. Burton (Oxford University Press)
The World of Insects, A. Zanetti (Sampson Low)
A Fieldguide to the Insects of Britain and Northern Europe, M. Chinery (Collins)
Larousse Encyclopedia of Animal Life, L. Bertin et al. (Hamlyn)
Insect Natural History, A. D. Imms (Collins)
Insect Life in the Tropics, T. W. Kirkpatrick (Longman)
An Introduction to the Study of Insects, D. J. Borror and D. M. DeLong (Holt, Rinehart and Winston)
Wildlife in House and Home, H. Mourier and O. Winding (Collins)
Towns and Gardens, D. F. Owen (Hodder and Stoughton)
The Natural History of the Garden, M. Chinery (Collins)
Fields and Lowlands, D. Boatman (Hodder and Stoughton)
Mountains and Moorlands, A. Darlington (Hodder and Stoughton)
Rivers, Lakes and Marshes, B. Whitton (Hodder and Stoughton)
The Pond, G. Thompson, J. Coldrey and G. Bernard (Collins)
Wildlife in Deserts, F. H. Wagner (Chanticleer)
Animal Ecology in Tropical Africa, D. F. Owen (Longman)
Animal Behavior, J. Alcock (Sinauer)
Animal Migration, O. von Frisch (Collins)
Feeding Strategy, J. Owen (Oxford University Press)
The Hunters, P. Whitfield and R. Orr (Hamlyn)
Camouflage and Mimicry, D. F. Owen (Oxford University Press)
Mimicry, W. Mickler (World University Library)
Defence in Animals, E. Edmunds (Longman)
Sexual Strategy, T. Halliday (Oxford University Press)
The Pollination of Flowers, M. Proctor and P. Yeo (Collins)
The Dictionary of Butterflies and Moths in Colour E. Laithwaite, A. Watson and P. E. S. Whalley (Michael Joseph)
Butterflies and Moths in Britain and Europe, D. Carter (British Museum (Natural History))
All Colour Book of Butterflies, R. Goodden (Octopus)
Social Insects, O. W. Richards (Harper)
The World of the Honeybee, C. G. Butler (Collins)
Bumblebee, J. B. Free and C. G. Butler (Collins)
Social Wasps, R. Edwards (Rentokil)

PART 2

MYSTERIES & MARVELS
OF THE
REPTILE WORLD

Ian Spellerberg and Marit McKerchar

Designed by Linda Sandey

Illustrated by David Quinn,
Craig Austin (Garden Studios),
Ian Jackson and Sam Thompson

Cartoons by John Shackell

The Arboreal Pit Viper's strong prehensile tail helps it climb trees.

The Red Bellied Turtle forages for food at the edge of the lake.

Contents

Jackson's Chameleon has three horns which may help in defence against predators, such as birds.

By using its large food pouch, the Monitor Lizard often swallows prey, such as a Palm Squirrel, whole.

The Galapagos Tortoise lives on the Island's lowlands and wanders along paths, which have been beaten by generations, to the highlands for food and water.

When disturbed by a predator, the small Royal Ball Python of West Africa throws itself into a ball-like coil, its head in the middle.

Introduction

Part Two is an exciting introduction to the world of reptiles. By looking at some of the more unusual, extraordinary and unexplained aspects of reptile life – how they move, track down and kill their food, care for their young – it provides a stimulating starting point for the study of this fascinating group of creatures.

Reptiles are "cold-blooded" and have to rely on their surroundings to keep their bodies at the right temperature, using various ways to warm up or cool down. They are unlike mammals which use food to heat themselves internally. All reptiles have scales which protect them from losing moisture through the skin and they all, including sea snakes, breathe air. Most lay eggs and these are always laid on land.

Reptiles are often feared as dangerous, slimy creatures. This section of the book introduces some very beautiful ones and will lead to an understanding of the variety and complexity of reptiles.

The Common Iguana is often found in tree tops up to 20m above the ground. If disturbed, it will drop to the ground from heights of up to 6m.

The young crocodile calls to its mother with piercing squeeks as it breaks out of its egg shell.

The striking eye-like patterns on the male Ocellated Gecko's back confuses its enemies.

TRUE or FALSE?

Look out for these questions and try to guess if they are true or false. The answers are on p. 64.

Warming up and keeping cool

Reptiles are 'cold-blooded' and they have to rely on their surroundings to keep their bodies at a temperature of 30-35°C. 'Warm-blooded' animals keep their bodies warm by using food as fuel for their internal 'burners'. This difference explains why warm-blooded animals need fairly regular meals while reptiles, such as snakes, can survive on one very large meal every few weeks or even once a year. The behaviour of many reptiles is the result of this need to stay at a steady temperature.

Winter store

Some lizards hiberate in winter, going into a long, cool sleep. They do not eat during this time but use fat stored in their bodies. The large, stumpy tail of the South Australian Shingleback lizard is thought to be a winter store of fat.

Shingleback Lizard

Its tail, which looks very much like its head, may also confuse enemies as they may attack the wrong end.

Dwarf Puff Adder

◄Cool hiding place

The Dwarf Puff Adder hides its body from the hot sun by burying itself in the desert sand. Only its eyes show above the surface. As well as keeping cool, the snake lies motionless for hours and even days, waiting to ambush small rodents and lizards which come close enough to provide a meal.

Dancing Lizards▼

The Fringe-Toed Lizard of Southwestern Africa 'dances' to keep cool. It lifts each foot in turn off the hot desert sand and sometimes raises all four feet at once, resting on its stomach. Like many other lizards, this lizard buries itself when the sun is at its hottest. Flaps over its ears and nose keep out the sand when it is underground.

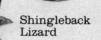

The long, fringed toes help the lizard to run very fast over soft, loose sand in the Namid Desert – one of the hottest places on earth.

Fringe-Toed Lizards

◀ A waterproof skin

One of the dangers of warming up by basking in the sun is that the heat can also dry out the body. Reptiles cope with this by having almost watertight skins, with no sweat glands through which water in their bodies could evaporate. The scales of crocodiles and alligators, called 'scutes' are much larger on their backs, making the skin more waterproof. The scales underneath, shaded from the sun are smaller and more flexible.

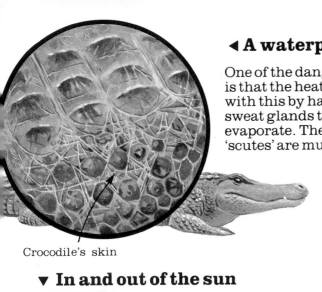

Crocodile's skin

▼ In and out of the sun

Each morning, before starting the days hunting for insects, spiders, worms and birds' eggs, the Jewelled Lizard lies in the sun to raise its temperature to 30-35°C. When warm, it is very active but soon becomes too hot. It then runs into the shade to cool down. For the rest of the day, it shuttles in and out of the sun to keep its body at the right temperature.

A Jewelled Lizard using the shade of a barrel cactus. Growing up to 75cm long, it can run very fast over sand and rocks.

TRUE or FALSE?

Skinks have anti-freeze in their blood.

Tuataras spend most of the day in their burrows but often lie in the sun in the morning and evening. They come out at night to hunt for insects and spiders but also eat worms and sails.

Cool character ▲

The Tuatara is a unique reptile, being able to survive on the small cold islands off New Zealand. Most reptiles live in warm areas as it is easier for them to cool down by keeping out of the sun than to warm up if the air is cold. The Tuatara is active at body temperatures lower than those of any other reptile and keeps its body at about 12°C.

As its body is so cool, this lizard is very slow. When moving, it breathes about once every seven seconds but this slows down to about once an hour when it is still. It also grows slowly taking 20 years to reach a length of about 60cm.

Super senses

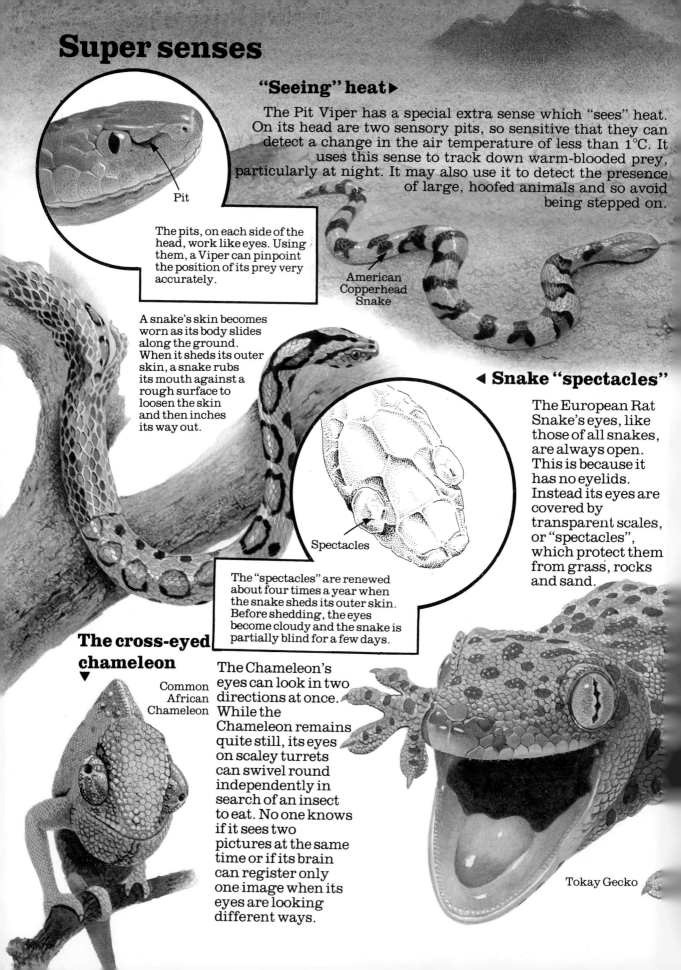

"Seeing" heat ▶

The Pit Viper has a special extra sense which "sees" heat. On its head are two sensory pits, so sensitive that they can detect a change in the air temperature of less than 1°C. It uses this sense to track down warm-blooded prey, particularly at night. It may also use it to detect the presence of large, hoofed animals and so avoid being stepped on.

Pit

The pits, on each side of the head, work like eyes. Using them, a Viper can pinpoint the position of its prey very accurately.

American Copperhead Snake

A snake's skin becomes worn as its body slides along the ground. When it sheds its outer skin, a snake rubs its mouth against a rough surface to loosen the skin and then inches its way out.

◀ Snake "spectacles"

The European Rat Snake's eyes, like those of all snakes, are always open. This is because it has no eyelids. Instead its eyes are covered by transparent scales, or "spectacles", which protect them from grass, rocks and sand.

Spectacles

The "spectacles" are renewed about four times a year when the snake sheds its outer skin. Before shedding, the eyes become cloudy and the snake is partially blind for a few days.

The cross-eyed chameleon
▼

Common African Chameleon

The Chameleon's eyes can look in two directions at once. While the Chameleon remains quite still, its eyes on scaley turrets can swivel round independently in search of an insect to eat. No one knows if it sees two pictures at the same time or if its brain can register only one image when its eyes are looking different ways.

Tokay Gecko

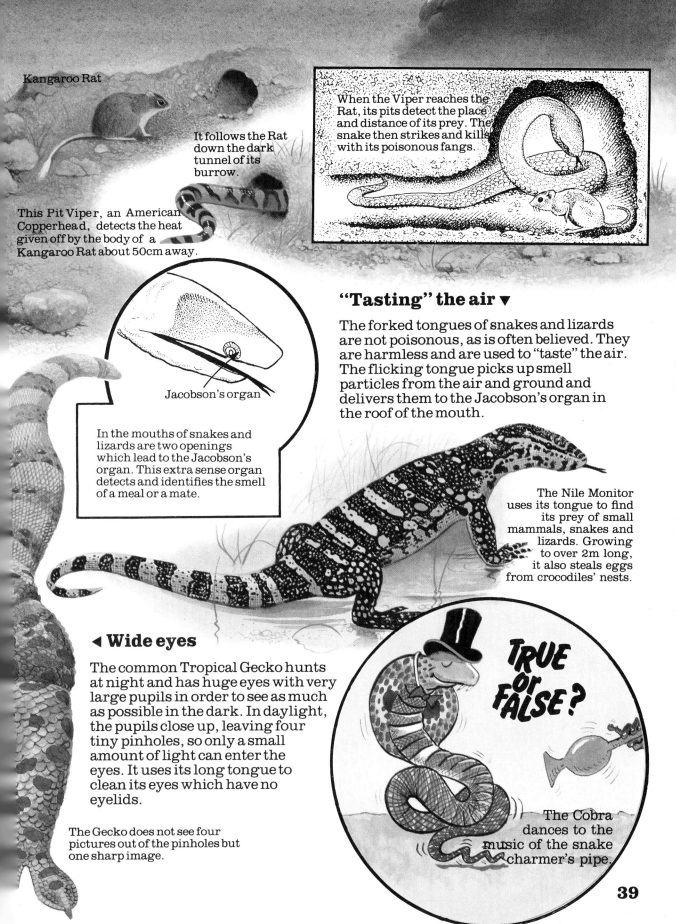

Kangaroo Rat

It follows the Rat down the dark tunnel of its burrow.

This Pit Viper, an American Copperhead, detects the heat given off by the body of a Kangaroo Rat about 50cm away.

When the Viper reaches the Rat, its pits detect the place and distance of its prey. The snake then strikes and kills with its poisonous fangs.

Jacobson's organ

In the mouths of snakes and lizards are two openings which lead to the Jacobson's organ. This extra sense organ detects and identifies the smell of a meal or a mate.

"Tasting" the air ▼

The forked tongues of snakes and lizards are not poisonous, as is often believed. They are harmless and are used to "taste" the air. The flicking tongue picks up smell particles from the air and ground and delivers them to the Jacobson's organ in the roof of the mouth.

The Nile Monitor uses its tongue to find its prey of small mammals, snakes and lizards. Growing to over 2m long, it also steals eggs from crocodiles' nests.

◀ Wide eyes

The common Tropical Gecko hunts at night and has huge eyes with very large pupils in order to see as much as possible in the dark. In daylight, the pupils close up, leaving four tiny pinholes, so only a small amount of light can enter the eyes. It uses its long tongue to clean its eyes which have no eyelids.

The Gecko does not see four pictures out of the pinholes but one sharp image.

TRUE or FALSE?

The Cobra dances to the music of the snake charmer's pipe.

39

Catching food

Catapult tongue ▼

During the day, the Chameleon moves slowly along the branches of trees in the forest hunting for insects and spiders to eat.

When near enough to its prey, it wraps its tail firmly round a twig, watching its target. Suddenly it shoots out its tongue, which stretches up to the length of its own body, with great accuracy. Then its tongue springs back into its mouth, bringing in the meal. The whole action takes less than a second.

Graceful Chameleon

The round end of the tongue acts like a suction pad and sticks to the prey. Back inside the mouth, the tongue is short and fat. It is like a sleeve of muscle round a long "launching bone" on the Chameleon's lower jaw.

Sticky suction pad

Launching bone

Causing a current

The Matamata Turtle lurks in the muddy rivers of Brazil. When small fish swim close, it opens its jaws so quickly that the fish are swept into its mouth by the current of water this makes.

Using its long neck, the turtle can hold its nostrils out of the water and breathe without moving and scaring the fish. Algae growing on the bumpy 40cm shell helps to camouflage the turtle.

Long tassels of skin look like weed and tempt passing fish to swim close.

False worm ▼

The Alligator Snapping Turtle's colours exactly match the muddy waters of the rivers in North America where it lives. It lies on the river bed with its mouth wide open, completely still except for its bright tongue which it wiggles to look like a worm. Hungry fish dart into its mouth after the "worm", the turtle snaps its jaws shut and swallows the fish. This turtle gets its name from its strong alligator-like tail and powerful jaws.

Weighing up to 100kg and 75cm long, this is the largest of the American fresh-water turtles.

Alligator Snapping Turtle.

Super swallowers ▼

The Boa Constrictor strikes its prey swiftly with its long, sharp teeth. The teeth slope backwards into the mouth so the more a victim struggles, the more firmly it is wedged on to them. The 2m Rainbow Boa suffocates its prey by squeezing it and then swallows it whole. A Boa, like all snakes, can swallow birds and other animals thicker than its own body because of its amazing jaw — the two halves move right apart at the hinge and are joined only by muscle.

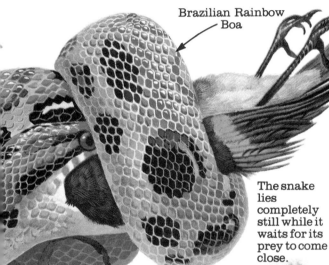

Brazilian Rainbow Boa

The snake lies completely still while it waits for its prey to come close.

A snorkel-like windpipe allows the snake to breathe while it swallows a large meal. A 7.5m Python was seen to eat a pig weighing about 54kg and later it swallowed a 47kg goat.

Egg eater

The African egg-eating snake lives in trees where it searches birds' nests hoping to find a meal of eggs. It often swallows eggs which are more than twice the width of its own body.

The snake stretches its elasticated jaws wide apart to fit round the egg, which it grips with its blunt teeth.

In its throat 30 special "teeth", which are extensions of the snake's spine, break the shell as the egg is swallowed. The egg white and yoke flow into the snake's stomach but the shell remains outside and is regurgitated.

Living larder ▶

The Australian Blind Snake lives in its larder — a termites' nest, where it feeds on its termite hosts. Surprisingly, the soldier termites do not often attack the snake. This may be because the snake smells like the termites and so goes unnoticed in the dark tunnels of the mound.

Compass Termites get their name from their mounds which they build in a north-south direction. The tower-like mounds are 3m high by 21m wide, but only 8-10cm thick. Their orientation helps reduce heat in summer but makes the most of winter sun.

The Blind Snake, about 40cm long, inside the termites' nest.

The snake's shiny skin acts like a smooth armour protecting it against bites from the termites' powerful jaws.

Fangs and poisons

Poisonous lizards

Of the 3,000 different kinds of lizards only two, the Gila Monster of North America and the Mexican Beaded Lizard, are poisonous. The Gila Monster does not have fangs to inject its poison. Instead, the venom flows from glands in its lower jaw on to grooves in its bottom teeth. When the Gila Monster bites its victim, venom washes around the teeth and is chewed into the wound. The potent venom acts on the victim's nerves and muscles causing internal bleeding and paralysis.

This "Monster" is only just over ½m long and weighs about 1½kg.

Gila Monster

Venomous vipers

The Viper's poison injecting fangs are so long that, when they are not being used, they hinge back against the roof of its mouth.

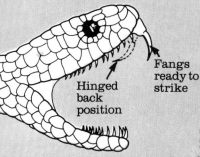

Hinged back position

Fangs ready to strike

The Viper's venom kills its prey by causing its blood to clot. This venom has been used in medicine to help cure blood diseases, such as haemophilia.

The Mongoose is one of the few animals which dares to confront a Cobra. It jumps close, before the Cobra strikes, and grabs the snake's head and jaw.

The Mongoose grips tightly with its teeth and can often win fights with small Cobras which have little chance of injecting their venom.

Spitting Cobra

The venom is squeezed out through holes at the tip of the fangs. It can spit about six times before the venom supply runs out, but this is replaced within a day.

The 2m long Spitting Cobra is found in many parts of Africa.

◄ The venom pistol

The Spitting Cobra squirts a fine stream of venom at its enemy's face, aiming for its eyes. The venom does not kill but it is painful and can make the victim blind. The venom can reach animals up to 3m away but the Cobra's shot is only accurate up to 2m. Using this "weapon" the Cobra can "warn off" its enemy from a safe distance.

King Cobra

Deadly babies

The long fangs of the Fer-de-Lance delivers very deadly venom. The young snakes are born alive in litters of 60-80 babies. Each baby is born complete with fangs and venom, making it dangerous from the start of life. They grow up to nearly 2m long.

The Fer-de-Lance was given its name because of its lance-shaped head and body. It lives in South America and the West Indies, where it is greatly feared because its search for rats and mice has brought it close to human homes.

Head of Fer-de-Lance

◀ The hooded cobra

The King Cobra is the largest poisonous snake, growing up to 5½m. Its tubular fangs stab directly into the victim when it strikes. They are connected to a venom gland which pumps poison through the fangs into the victim. When disturbed, the Cobra raises its body into the strike position, its neck stretched into a threatening hood. Its venom is lethal to most animals, and its fangs deliver more venom than any other snake — one bite can kill an elephant in four hours.

African Boomslang — about 1m long.

Boomslangs have the most deadly poison of any rear-fanged snake, but they rarely bite people as they are shy, hiding away in the trees.

A back-fanged killer ▶

Some snakes, such as the Boomslang, have fangs at the back of their mouths rather than at the front.

Chameleon

The short, fragile fangs are set well back in the upper jaw.

TRUE or FALSE?

Snakes have been used as weapons of war.

When the Boomslang attacks its prey it needs to hold on with its mouth and chew the victim's flesh in order to inject a large dose of venom. This way of poisoning is not as efficient as the speedy strike of front-fanged snakes, but the Boomslang's venom, when injected, is just as deadly.

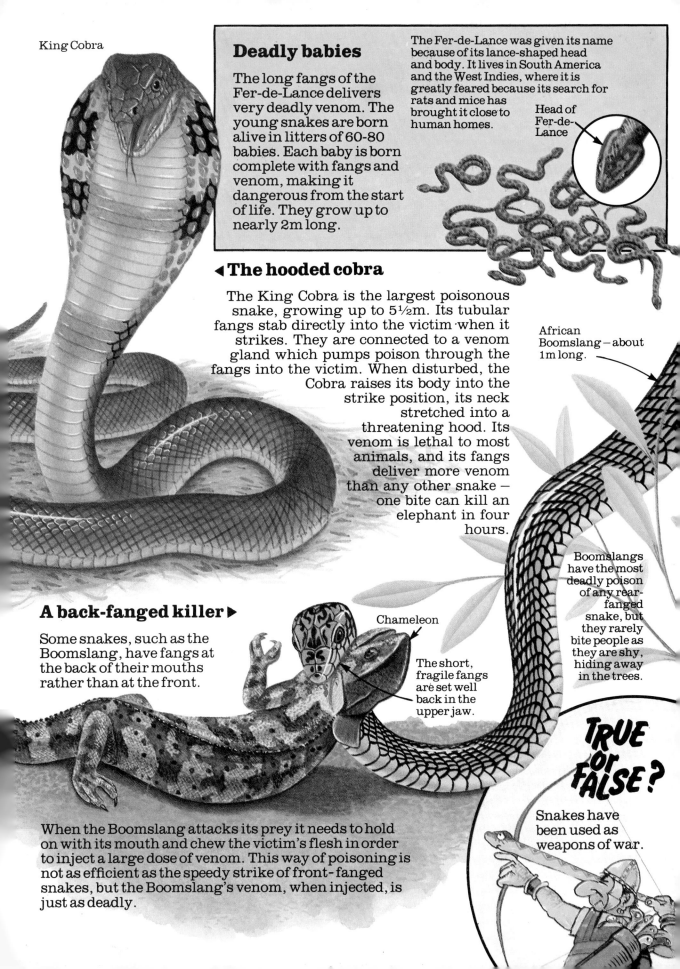

Escape and defence

If cornered by an enemy, this lizard makes a threatening display. It stretches out the spiny pouch round its throat, making its head look twice its normal size. It expands its body, opens its mouth to show the bright colours inside and hisses, but it rarely bites.

Bearded Lizard

The lizard, which is over 50cm long, uses its long tail to balance when running fast on two legs.

A two-legged escape

The Bearded Lizard of Australia escapes from predators by running away on its hind legs. This is a mystery because it travels faster on all fours. It may be that, as running makes it very hot, it can keep cooler by holding its body upright in the air, above the hot ground.

A shell fortress ▶

The tortoise carries its shell fortress on its back. The shell is made of horny plates, strengthened underneath by bone so that the tortoise's body is enclosed in a box which can resist almost any attack. It can withdraw its head and legs into this box when danger threatens. Under its stomach is another plate of shell, called the plastron, which in some tortoises hinges in the middle. The Box Tortoise can draw up each end of this plate tightly against the top shell, called the carapace.

Radiated Tortoise of Madagascar

This defence is so effective that tortoises and turtles have survived, almost unchanged, for over 200 million years. Not all of them can withdraw into their shells — the Big-Headed Turtle's head, as its name suggests, can not be withdrawn, and the Snake-Necked Turtle bends its neck sideways, along its shell, to tuck it out of sight.

Stinkpot

The tiny, 10cm Stinkpot is North America's smallest water turtle. As well as its shell, it has a second line of defence against predators, such as crows. When disturbed it gives off a terrible smell from special musk glands. This turtle can climb well and the female usually lays her eggs in nests dug on land.

Musk Turtles spend most of their time in pools and sluggish streams. They feed on water insects, tadpoles, snails and fish and often also take fishermen's bait from the end of lines.

◀ Quick change artist

The Chameleon can change the colour and pattern of its skin in order to improve its camouflage in trees where it hunts for insects and is preyed on by snakes. It does this by means of special yellow, black and reflecting white colour cells in its skin. Colour changes are probably controlled by the Chameleon's nervous system which is triggered by light changes as well as by its emotions, such as fear.

African Chameleon

Skin

Yellow cells

Melanophores

Reflecting cells

Shading is controlled by melanophores which move the dark pigment between the layers of skin.

The colour cells change in size which varies the concentrations of different colours so a new colour is produced.

TRUE or FALSE?

Chameleons turn black with rage.

Coiled defence▼

To escape from a predator this small, 21cm, slow-moving lizard hides in a rock crevice. Here it curls up, stuffing the tip of its tail into its mouth, to make a tight ball, protecting its soft stomach.

Armadillo Lizard of South Africa

The lizard lies completely still until the danger has passed. A bony layer in the armour-like skin on its head and back makes it rock hard. Unlike most lizards, the Armadillo's tail does not break off easily when pulled.

45

The art of bluff

Many reptiles defend themselves by deceiving their enemy in some unusual and curious ways.

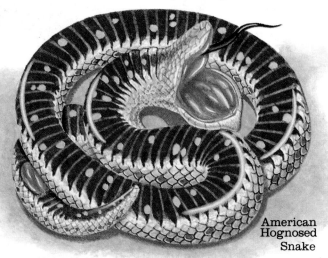

American Hognosed Snake

The inside of the snake's mouth looks like rotting meat and the snake gives off a terrible smell which helps to convince its enemy that it is dead.

◄ Instant death

The Hognosed Snake imitates a Rattlesnake when it meets an enemy. It raises its head and rubs its tail against the side of its body to make a rattling sound. If this does not frighten off the enemy, the snake rolls on to its back and pretends to be dead, lying completely still with its mouth open. Surprisingly, a mammal or bird is usually taken in by this sham, although it saw that the snake was alive only a moment before. Most of them will not eat the flesh of long-dead animals as its tastes unpleasant and could be poisonous.

Snake look-alikes

The Milk Snake protects itself from attack by looking very like the poisonous Coral Snake. The brightly coloured bands on the Coral Snake's body alerts mammals of its poisonous nature. By copying this pattern, the Milk Snake is also thought to be poisonous even though it is quite harmless.

Coral Snake

Milk Snake

The model for the mimic is one of the less poisonous of the many Coral Snakes. Because mammals survive encounters with them, they remember and learn to avoid them in future. The Milk Snake can be told apart from the Coral Snake, as in the rhyme:

Red and black, friend of Jack,
Red and yellow, kill a fellow.

This lizard can hardly be seen against the pebbles—its markings, irregular shape and a line along its spine divides up its body and disguises its shape.

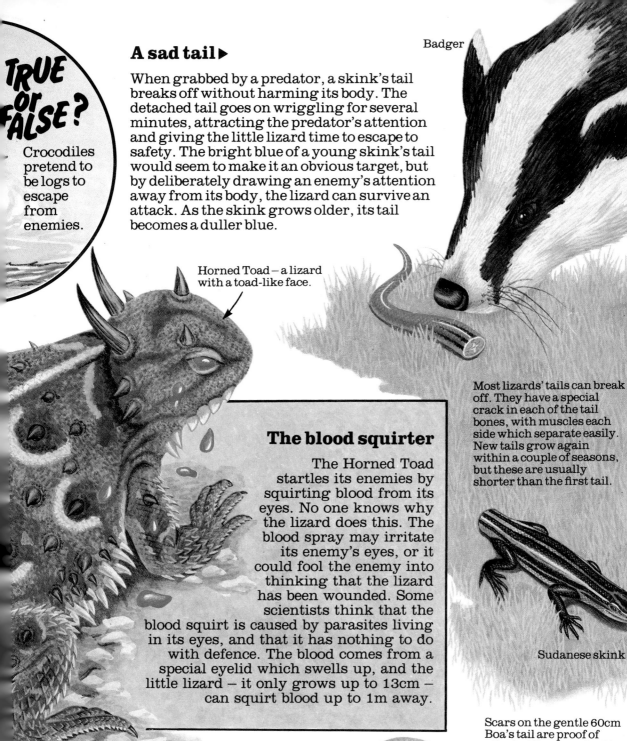

A sad tail ▶

When grabbed by a predator, a skink's tail breaks off without harming its body. The detached tail goes on wriggling for several minutes, attracting the predator's attention and giving the little lizard time to escape to safety. The bright blue of a young skink's tail would seem to make it an obvious target, but by deliberately drawing an enemy's attention away from its body, the lizard can survive an attack. As the skink grows older, its tail becomes a duller blue.

Badger

Horned Toad – a lizard with a toad-like face.

The blood squirter

The Horned Toad startles its enemies by squirting blood from its eyes. No one knows why the lizard does this. The blood spray may irritate its enemy's eyes, or it could fool the enemy into thinking that the lizard has been wounded. Some scientists think that the blood squirt is caused by parasites living in its eyes, and that it has nothing to do with defence. The blood comes from a special eyelid which swells up, and the little lizard – it only grows up to 13cm – can squirt blood up to 1m away.

Most lizards' tails can break off. They have a special crack in each of the tail bones, with muscles each side which separate easily. New tails grow again within a couple of seasons, but these are usually shorter than the first tail.

Sudanese skink

Scars on the gentle 60cm Boa's tail are proof of attacks it has survived by using this clever bluff.

Rubber Boa of Mexico and southwestern U.S.A.

Two-faced snake ▶

When the Rubber Boa is disturbed by an enemy, it coils into a tight ball and hides its head under its body. It raises instead its blunt head-like tail and waves it aggressively at its enemy. If the enemy attacks, it will go for what it thinks is the snake's head, while the real head remains safely hidden.

Frills and decorations

Disappearing act ▶

The Leaf-Tailed Gecko of Madagasca is
almost impossible to spot, even when
seen close to, against the bark of trees
where it lives. Its unusual tail, dappled
colours and the fringe of scales along its
sides and legs give it perfect camouflage.
It can curl its tail round to hold on to
branches and its huge eyes are useful
when hunting at night.

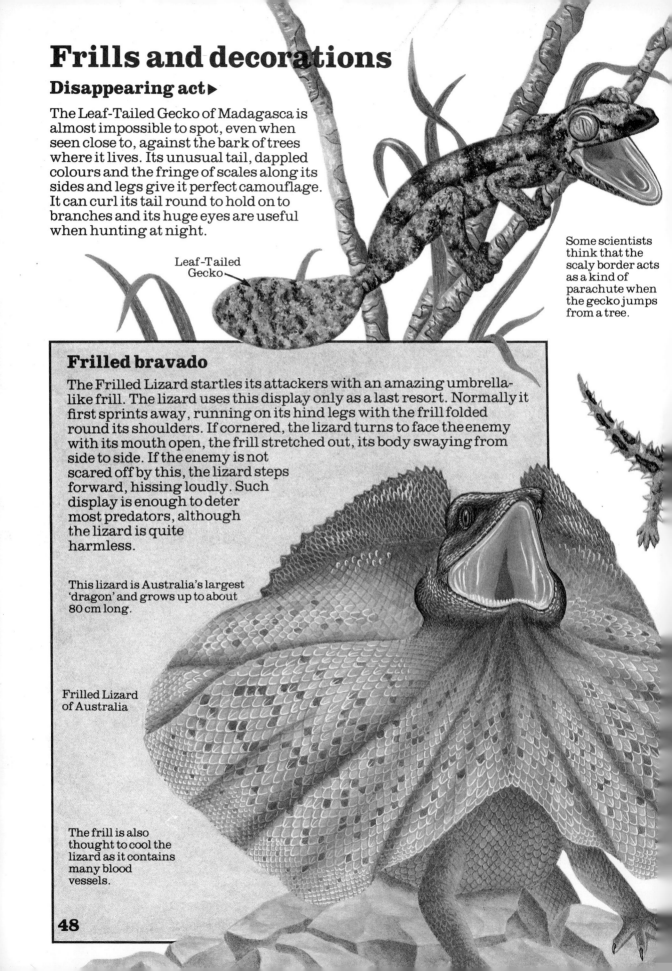

Leaf-Tailed
Gecko

Some scientists
think that the
scaly border acts
as a kind of
parachute when
the gecko jumps
from a tree.

Frilled bravado

The Frilled Lizard startles its attackers with an amazing umbrella-
like frill. The lizard uses this display only as a last resort. Normally it
first sprints away, running on its hind legs with the frill folded
round its shoulders. If cornered, the lizard turns to face the enemy
with its mouth open, the frill stretched out, its body swaying from
side to side. If the enemy is not
scared off by this, the lizard steps
forward, hissing loudly. Such
display is enough to deter
most predators, although
the lizard is quite
harmless.

This lizard is Australia's largest
'dragon' and grows up to about
80 cm long.

Frilled Lizard
of Australia

The frill is also
thought to cool the
lizard as it contains
many blood
vessels.

48

Threatening throat ▶

The male Anole defends his territory against other males by extending his brilliant throat sac. A smaller lizard will retreat immediately but anoles of the same size may display to each other for several hours.

The two males sidle round each other with their bodies puffed up. Then one, followed by the other raises his body off the ground, stretches his throat sac and wags his tail up and down. After a few minutes, they both drop down before starting again. Usually they rarely fight and eventually lose interest in each other and walk away.

Male anole displaying his throat sac.

The display of the throat is also a sign of courtship to a female anole. The sac is usually folded against the anole's throat otherwise it would be easily spotted by hawks and other predators.

Thorny devil

The Moloch is a very prickly mouthful for a predator. Its body is covered with a mass of spikes as sharp as thorns. Apart from protecting this 15cm lizard, the spikes are very useful in the hot, dry desert as they collect water. Dew condenses on them and runs along tiny grooves in the Moloch's skin and into its mouth. This enables it to live for months without drinking.

Australian Moloch

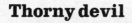

Although it looks so fierce, the Moloch is quite harmless and eats only ants. It sits by an ant trail, flicking out its tongue and picking up 20 or 30 in a minute. One meal can consist of up to 1,500 ants which it crushes with its cheek teeth.

Rattle alarm ▶

The Rattlesnake warns intruders by sounding its alarm rattle. This gives an approaching animal time to escape and also saves the snake from being stepped on by large, hoofed animals. The rattle is made of loosely linked scaley sections which are the remains of the tail each time the snake sheds its skin. To sound the alarm, the snake vibrates its tail about 50 times a minute and the noise can be heard up to 30 metres away.

The snake sheds its skin three or four times a year, adding a new section to its tail each time. But the rattle cannot be used to tell the snake's age because the older ones start to wear off when there are about eight.

Rattle

Timber Rattlesnake of North America

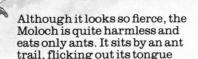

Courtship

During the mating season, many male reptiles try to attract females with impressive displays. They also fight other males for mates and for territory.

Monitor wrestlers▶

Male Monitor Lizards wrestle at the beginning of the mating season for female lizards. Surprisingly, neither male is hurt in these fights, although they are armed with sharp teeth and claws and strong tails. It seems that the wrestling is more a trial of strength than an attempt to kill each other — each lizard tries to push the other to the ground, and the first one to succeed wins the female.

The Two-Banded Monitor grows up to 3m long and is one of the largest lizards in the world. The gentlemanly mock battles only occur in the mating season. The Monitors do have very fierce fights over food which often result in bad injuries.

Two-Banded Monitor Lizard

Battering ram

The courtship of Greek Tortoises takes place in warm weather when they are able to move fairly quickly — up to 4.5km per hour, which is about the same speed as a man walking. The male chases his chosen female, and when he catches her he starts to butt her from behind, using his head like a battering ram. At the same time he bites her back legs quite fiercely. This onslaught makes the female draw her head and legs into the shell, and mating then takes place.

If the male cannot find a female during the breeding season, he has been known to butt anything in sight, from flower pots to people.

The male hisses while butting the female

Greek Tortoises — about 30cm long.

TRUE or FALSE?

Boas tickle their mates

Cheek caressing▶

In spring and early summer, the Painted Turtle male seeks out females and makes an attempt to court any one he comes across. He swims quickly after the female, overtakes, and turns to face her head on. She continues to swim on so the male is pushed backwards. In this face to face position, the male gently strokes the female's cheeks with his long foreclaws. If the female is receptive, she sinks to the bottom of the pond and allows the male to mate with her.

Common Night Adders of Africa grow 70-90cm long.

The female lays between 12 and 24 eggs which take up to 4 months to hatch.

◀ A love dance

Early in spring, Night Adders dance together as a prelude to mating. The male approaches the female from behind and rubs his chin and throat over her tail. He slowly jerks forward, moving himself along her body. After a while, the female slows down and throws her body in loops with the male following every move. He then wraps his tail around her body and twists, ready to mate.

Splashing out

Before courting starts, the male Nile Crocodile fights with other males to establish a breeding territory on the river bank. The male then patrols the patch of water close to the beach, bellowing at any rival male and fighting off intruders. When a female approaches, he gives off a strong smell of musk and roars. He claps his jaws and lashes his tail, sending clouds of spray all around. He swims in smaller and smaller circles round the female until he is close enough for them to mate.

The female choses a male with a territory which has good sunbathing and nest sites on the bank. She calls him with deep, husky noises.

Male Nile Crocodile

Female Painted Turtles grow to over 15cm long and are considerably larger than the 11cm males. Only males have long foreclaws.

Painted Turtles

Eggs and nurseries

Most reptiles lay eggs, although a few species do give birth to live young. All the ones that hatch from eggs have a special "tool" for breaking out of their shells; snakes and lizards have a sharp egg tooth, while tortoises and crocodiles have a horny knob on the end of their snouts.

Green Tree Python of New Guinea

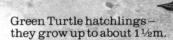

Green Turtle hatchlings – they grow up to about 1½m.

The baby Pythons are born yellow or red and change to the rich green colour of the adult snakes when they are about 1m long. Adults grow up to about 2m.

Body warmers

Three to four months after mating, the female python lays up to 100 eggs. She gathers the eggs into a pile and coils her body around them for about three months until they hatch. By a special kind of shivering, the mother python can raise her body temperature by about 8°C while she incubates the eggs – an unusual ability in "cold-blooded" animals. She only leaves her eggs for occasional visits to the water and for rare meals.

Caring crocodiles ▶

Each year, the female Nile Crocodile lays up to 40 eggs in a nest dug in the sand above the waterline on the riverbank. She builds the nest in a shady place, about 20-30cm deep, so that the eggs keep at an even temperature – not varying more than 3°C. She covers the eggs with sand and both parents guard them during the 90 days incubation. Predators, such as the Nile Monitor, have a taste for crocodile eggs.

When it is ready to hatch, the young crocodile makes loud piping calls. Its mother scrapes away the sand covering the eggs, gently picks up each baby with her teeth, and carries them in a special pouch at the bottom of her mouth to a "nursery" pool area off the river. The young crocodiles follow their mother about like ducklings and crawl over her face and back.

The young crocodile stays in the "nursery" for about two months, guarded by its parents.

The first few steps of the Turtle's life are its most dangerous – it has to find its way to the sea past hungry crabs and Frigate Birds. The Turtles have more chance of reaching the sea if they make the dash together. Somehow the young Turtles know which direction to go when they leave their nests. They may follow the sound of the waves or head for the brighter light which is reflected off the sea.

Obstacle course ▲

The female Green Turtle lays her eggs in the sand dunes on the beaches of Ascension Island where they are incubated by the heat of the sun. She digs a nest with her hind flippers and, after laying about 100 eggs, covers them with sand and lumbers back to the sea. The male Turtle waits for her offshore, and they mate again and produce two or three more batches of eggs in the mating year. They usually return to the breeding grounds only once every three years.

On a limb

Most chameleon's bury their parchment-like eggs underground and the babies then hatch about eight months later. The Dwarf Chameleon's eggs develop inside the mother's body and she gives birth to about 16 eggs which hatch almost immediately. The mother places each sticky egg carefully on a twig or leaf as they are laid. The young Chameleon then wriggles and twists its way out of the soft egg shell.

The baby Dwarf Chameleon is only 3-4cm long, but it starts to hunt for insects within a few hours of being born. Adults grow up to 20cm.

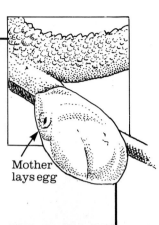

Mother lays egg

Egg sticks to twig

Chameleon twists out of the egg

The Nile Crocodile grows over 6m long.

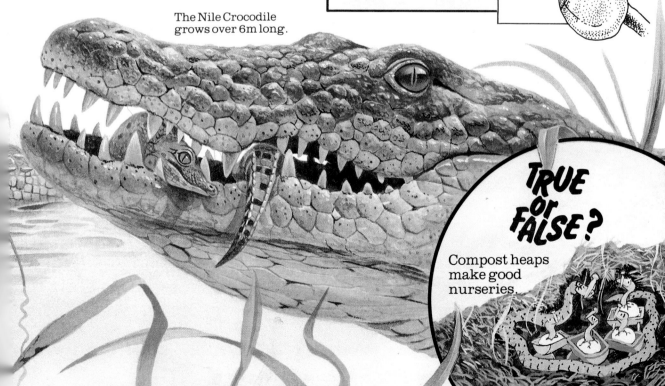

TRUE or FALSE?

Compost heaps make good nurseries.

On the move

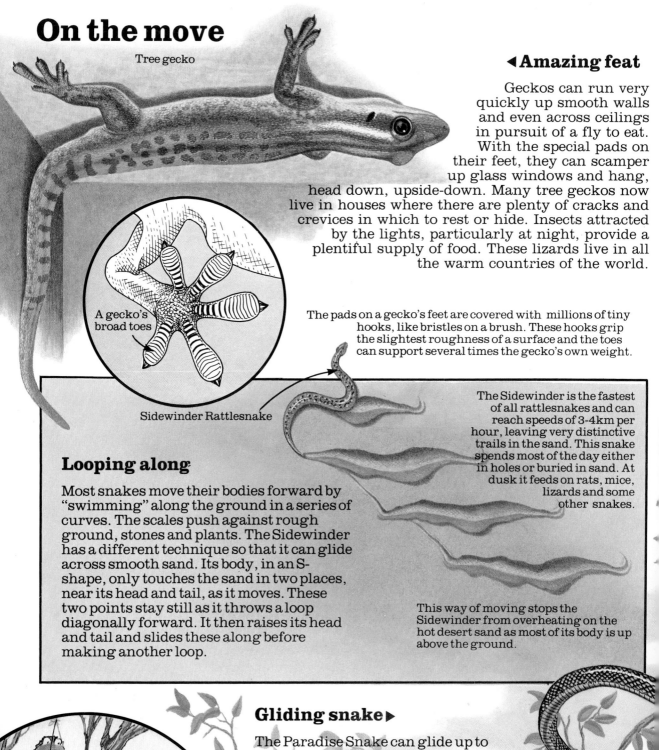

Tree gecko

◄ Amazing feat

Geckos can run very quickly up smooth walls and even across ceilings in pursuit of a fly to eat. With the special pads on their feet, they can scamper up glass windows and hang, head down, upside-down. Many tree geckos now live in houses where there are plenty of cracks and crevices in which to rest or hide. Insects attracted by the lights, particularly at night, provide a plentiful supply of food. These lizards live in all the warm countries of the world.

A gecko's broad toes

The pads on a gecko's feet are covered with millions of tiny hooks, like bristles on a brush. These hooks grip the slightest roughness of a surface and the toes can support several times the gecko's own weight.

Sidewinder Rattlesnake

The Sidewinder is the fastest of all rattlesnakes and can reach speeds of 3-4km per hour, leaving very distinctive trails in the sand. This snake spends most of the day either in holes or buried in sand. At dusk it feeds on rats, mice, lizards and some other snakes.

Looping along

Most snakes move their bodies forward by "swimming" along the ground in a series of curves. The scales push against rough ground, stones and plants. The Sidewinder has a different technique so that it can glide across smooth sand. Its body, in an S-shape, only touches the sand in two places, near its head and tail, as it moves. These two points stay still as it throws a loop diagonally forward. It then raises its head and tail and slides these along before making another loop.

This way of moving stops the Sidewinder from overheating on the hot desert sand as most of its body is up above the ground.

Gliding snake ►

The Paradise Snake can glide up to 35m from one tree to another. It launches itself from a branch, keeping its body in a S-shape and uses its tail like a rudder. By hollowing its body, it traps a cushion of air underneath which acts as a parachute and slows down its fall on to a lower branch.

TRUE or FALSE?

Crocodiles climb trees.

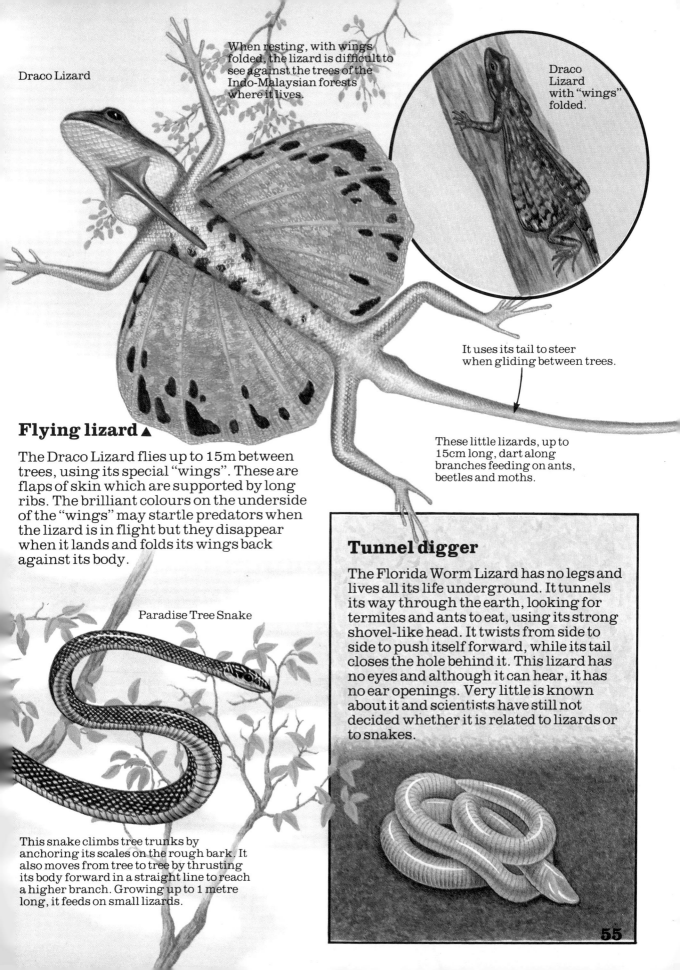

Draco Lizard

When resting, with wings folded, the lizard is difficult to see against the trees of the Indo-Malaysian forests where it lives.

Draco Lizard with "wings" folded.

It uses its tail to steer when gliding between trees.

Flying lizard ▲

The Draco Lizard flies up to 15m between trees, using its special "wings". These are flaps of skin which are supported by long ribs. The brilliant colours on the underside of the "wings" may startle predators when the lizard is in flight but they disappear when it lands and folds its wings back against its body.

These little lizards, up to 15cm long, dart along branches feeding on ants, beetles and moths.

Paradise Tree Snake

This snake climbs tree trunks by anchoring its scales on the rough bark. It also moves from tree to tree by thrusting its body forward in a straight line to reach a higher branch. Growing up to 1 metre long, it feeds on small lizards.

Tunnel digger

The Florida Worm Lizard has no legs and lives all its life underground. It tunnels its way through the earth, looking for termites and ants to eat, using its strong shovel-like head. It twists from side to side to push itself forward, while its tail closes the hole behind it. This lizard has no eyes and although it can hear, it has no ear openings. Very little is known about it and scientists have still not decided whether it is related to lizards or to snakes.

Taking to the water

Walking on the water ▶

The Basilisk Lizard escapes from its enemies by dropping on to the water from river-side trees or bushes. It then runs, at speeds up to 12kph, across the top of the water. It moves so fast on the long, fringed toes on its back legs that it does not have time to sink. If it does slow down, the lizard breaks through the surface of the water and swims, partly submerged, for the rest of its journey.

The Basilisk Lizard is called the Jésus Christo lizard in South America because it runs on water.

The Basilisk is named after the crested lizard which, according to the legend, hatched from an egg laid by a cockerel and could kill anything with just one glance. This iguanid lizard, which grows up to 60cm long, is quite harmless and feeds on plants and insects in tropical America.

The Anaconda can swim fast and often feeds on fish, turtles and even caimans.

The snake eats its prey whole. A 7m Anaconda was reported to have swallowed a 2m caiman – a meal which would have lasted the snake for several weeks.

◀ A swimming serpent

The Anaconda spends most of its day lying in the sluggish rivers or swamps of tropical South America, or sunbathing on low trees. At dusk it waits for its prey, usually birds and small mammals, to come down to the water to drink. Then it grabs its victim in its mouth and quickly loops its body round it. The snake slowly tightens its coils until its prey can no longer breathe and dies of suffocation, or drags it into the water to drown before eating it.

Submarine reptiles ▶

The Hawksbill Turtle, which lives in tropical seas around the world, has a light-weight shell and paddle-like legs. It uses its front legs to swim slowly through the water and its back legs to steer, like a rudder. The female Hawksbill crawls clumsily on land when she comes out to lay her eggs while the male rarely leaves the water.

Stone ballast ▼

The Gharial is a long, slender-snouted crocodile which lives in
Indian rivers. It spends much of its time lying in the water with
only its eyes and nostrils above the surface. Like all crocodiles,
the Gharial swallows stones to help it stay under the water.
Without this extra weight, young crocodiles become top heavy
and would tip over. The Gharial can stay under the water for
over an hour. It has special flaps which cover its nostrils and a
valve which shuts off its windpipe so it can open its mouth to
catch fish without swallowing lots of water.

TRUE or FALSE?

Crocodiles cry
when eating
their victims.

The lump on the end
of some adults' snouts
is a mystery. It may
increase the noise of
the mating call but no
one really knows.

The Gharial's
snout has over 100
sharp, even, teeth
which it uses to
catch fish.

The Hawksbill has
always been
hunted for its shell.
Although plastics
have largely
replaced tortoise-
shell, this turtle is
still in danger of
extinction.

The turtle eats water plants,
sea urchins, fish and crabs. Its
flesh is sometimes poisonous
to human beings, perhaps
because it also eats stinging
jelly fish and Portuguese
men-of-war.

Underwater grazing grounds

The Marine Iguana of the Galapagos Islands is the
only lizard which is at home in the sea. There is little
food on the barren volcanic shores and the lizard
goes to sea for its meals of seaweed. When the tide
goes out, exposing the reefs and algae-covered
rocks, it plunges into the cool water. Clinging to the
rocks with its sharp claws, it tears off the seaweed
with its mouth. Some iguanas may swim out beyond
the surf and dive down 5m to feed on the seabed, each
dive lasting about 15 minutes.

Before diving into the
cool sea, iguanas
warm themselves in
the sun. To avoid over-
heating, they hold
their bodies off the hot
rocks or face the sun,
so their heads provide
shade for their bodies.

Marine Iguanas
on Hood Island.

A place to live

Bird perch▼

Many snakes spend their lives in trees. The African Vine Snake lies along the branch of a tree with the front part of its 1.5m body held out stiffly in space. It stays motionless for hours, its long, slender body looking like a small branch to an unwary bird. It can move very fast through the trees, as well as on the ground, looking for meals of small birds and lizards.

Ruby-Topaz Hummingbird

The tiny Ruby-Topaz Hummingbird hovers near the snake, its wings beating 50-80 times a second.

The Vine Snake keeps its tongue quite still, instead of flicking it in and out like most snakes. It is thought that it may use its tongue as a bait to attract its prey.

African Vine Snake

At home in the sea

The Olive Sea Snake spends its life in warm, tropical Asian seas. Here it eats, breeds and produces live young, never leaving the water to go ashore. The snake's body is flat and its tail acts like an oar, driving it through the water. The snake breathes air and with special lungs, almost the length of its body, it can stay underwater for up to two hours. Flaps cover its nostrils when it is submerged. It can also "breathe" in air from the sea through its skin in much the same way as a fish "breathes" through its gills.

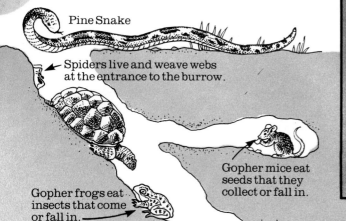

Pine Snake

Spiders live and weave webs at the entrance to the burrow.

Gopher frogs eat insects that come or fall in.

Gopher mice eat seeds that they collect or fall in.

Cave crickets feed on beetle dung.

Beetles feed on the tortoise's dung.

Shared shelter▲

The Gopher Tortoise digs its own home, a long, cool tunnel, amongst the sand hills of southern parts of the United States. Here it can escape during the day from the heat of the sun and it shares the burrow with several other animals. They all live together quite happily, each with its own place and habits. The tortoise can defend its home against unwelcome visitors, such as a Pine Snake, by blocking the entrance with its shell.

TRUE or FALSE?

Alligators live in sewers

Home of many lizards ▶

Most species of anoles live in trees, clinging to the branches with their long toes. They are found only in the Americas and particularly in the West Indies. In Cuba several kinds of these lizards live together in the same group of trees.

The 45cm Giant Anole lives in the tree tops where it hunts for frogs and young birds. A medium anole, 16cm long, lives on the tree trunks, while a third, slender anole, less than 13cm long, makes its home on the ground at the bottom of the trees.

Giant Anole

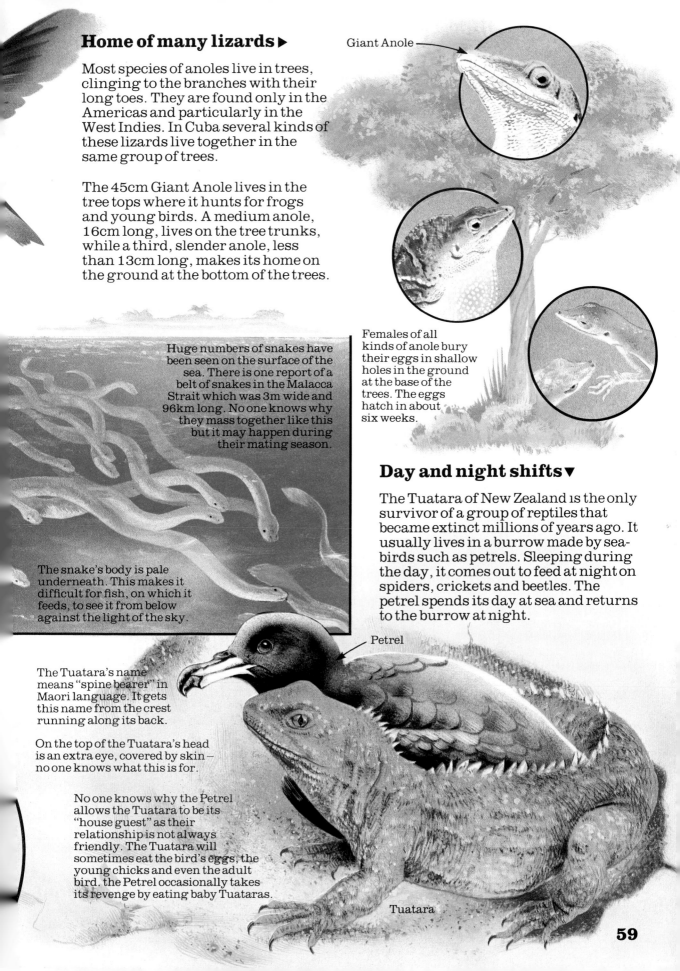

Females of all kinds of anole bury their eggs in shallow holes in the ground at the base of the trees. The eggs hatch in about six weeks.

Huge numbers of snakes have been seen on the surface of the sea. There is one report of a belt of snakes in the Malacca Strait which was 3m wide and 96km long. No one knows why they mass together like this but it may happen during their mating season.

The snake's body is pale underneath. This makes it difficult for fish, on which it feeds, to see it from below against the light of the sky.

Day and night shifts ▼

The Tuatara of New Zealand is the only survivor of a group of reptiles that became extinct millions of years ago. It usually lives in a burrow made by sea-birds such as petrels. Sleeping during the day, it comes out to feed at night on spiders, crickets and beetles. The petrel spends its day at sea and returns to the burrow at night.

Petrel

The Tuatara's name means "spine bearer" in Maori language. It gets this name from the crest running along its back.

On the top of the Tuatara's head is an extra eye, covered by skin — no one knows what this is for.

No one knows why the Petrel allows the Tuatara to be its "house guest" as their relationship is not always friendly. The Tuatara will sometimes eat the bird's eggs, the young chicks and even the adult bird, the Petrel occasionally takes its revenge by eating baby Tuataras.

Tuatara

Curious events

Living toothbrush ▶

During the heat of the day, the crocodile lies on a muddy bank with its mouth wide open. Water evaporates from its mouth, cooling it down, rather like a dog panting when hot. Plovers land on its jaw to peck food from its teeth. They seem to be in no danger. This may be because they clean the crocodile's teeth, which it cannot do itself as its tongue is not moveable. The birds may also remove leeches and other irritating insects.

No one knows why the inside of its mouth is such a brilliant colour, but the crocodile may use it as a shock tactic – suddenly opening its mouth and freezing its prey with terror.

Spur-winged Plover.

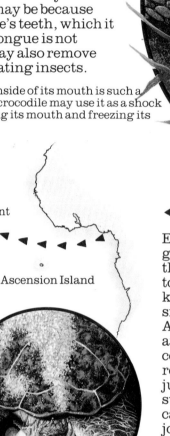

Current

Ascension Island

The Female Green Turtle lays her eggs in a hole over 50cm deep which she scoops out with her hind flippers.

◀ Long distance swimmers

Every three years, groups of Green Turtles gather together and swim 2,000km from their grazing grounds off the coast of Brazil to lay their eggs on Ascension Island. No one knows how the Turtles manage to find the small 13km by 9km island in the middle of the Atlantic. There is an ocean current running at just under 2km per hour from the African coast, past Ascension Island, to Brazil. To return to their grazing grounds the Turtles just have to drift with this. But as their swimming speed is only 2km per hour, they cannot go against the current on the outward journey and must find another route. Scientists think that they either follow smells given off by different parts of the sea, or navigate by means of the sun and stars. The round trip takes about three years.

Snake eats snake ▶

When a Rattlesnake comes across a King Snake it acts in a very unusual way. Instead of preparing to strike with its poison-injecting fangs, the rattler keeps its head as far as possible from the King Snake and uses the middle of its body to try to beat it off. The King Snake, not put off, grasps the rattler's neck in its teeth, wraps its body round the rattler and chokes it to death. The non-poisonous King Snake is successful in these battles because it is immune to the rattler's, usually lethal, poison.

The King Snake also attacks and eats other King Snakes.

A two-headed serpent ▶

Occasionally freak two-headed snakes are born. A two-headed King Snake which lived in San Diego Zoo was always in danger because of the King Snake's habit of eating other snakes. One night one of the heads tried to swallow the other. The attacked head was rescued in the morning by a keeper, but it later tried to take its revenge on the first head and this attack killed both heads and their one body.

The two-headed snake of San Diego Zoo also had two lungs, instead of one, and two hearts.

Rafts ▼

Scientists think that the reptiles on the Galapagos Islands reached there by means of natural rafts from the coast of Equador, 800-900km away. A tortoise, for example, would climb on to a piece of drift wood to rest, which then drifted out to sea.

Mammals are less able than reptiles to cope with the lack of food and water on rafts, and the Rice Rats are the only native land mammals which exist on the Galapagos Islands.

Stowaways ▶

Geckos living in ports quite often find their way on to ships while searching for insect meals. They have travelled to remote parts of the world on these ships as "stowaways" – the Turkish Gecko has migrated to most of the world's main tropical areas in this way.

California King Snake.

It swallows the Rattlesnake by "walking" its mouth and body over the dead snake.

TRUE or FALSE?

Snakes can jump a meter high.

Record breakers

The biggest meal

The biggest meal recorded was an Impala weighing nearly 60kg found in the stomach of a 4.87m African Rock Python.

Smallest snakes

Thread Snakes are only 1 to 1.3cm long and are so thin they could glide through the hole left in a normal pencil if the lead was removed.

The most deaths

In India, Indian Cobras kill about 7,500 people per year which is about 25% of all the snake bite deaths in India.

Fastest snake

The Black Mamba can reach speeds of 25km per hour in short bursts. It races along with its head and the front of its body raised, mouth open and tongue flicking.

Tiny but loud

The Least Geckos are the smallest reptiles at only 2½cm long. Some of these tiny lizards sing in loud chirrups, which can be heard up to 10km away and attract mates.

The largest reptile

Salt-water Crocodiles are today's largest reptiles. They grow to an average of 4½m long, although there have been reports of larger beasts. A 8m Crocodile was killed in 1954 which was over 1.5m tall at the shoulder and would have weighed nearly 2 tons.

The longest starvation

The Okinawa Habu Snake of the West Pacific can survive for more than 3 years without food.

The longest fangs

The highly venomous Gaboon Viper of Tropical Africa has the longest fangs of any snake. One 1.2m snake had fangs nearly 3cm long. It will only bite if really provoked.

Fastest swimming snake

The Yellow-bellied Sea Snake of the Indo-Pacific region can swim at the rate of 1m per second. Sea Snakes can also dive 100m deep and stay under water for up to 5 hours.

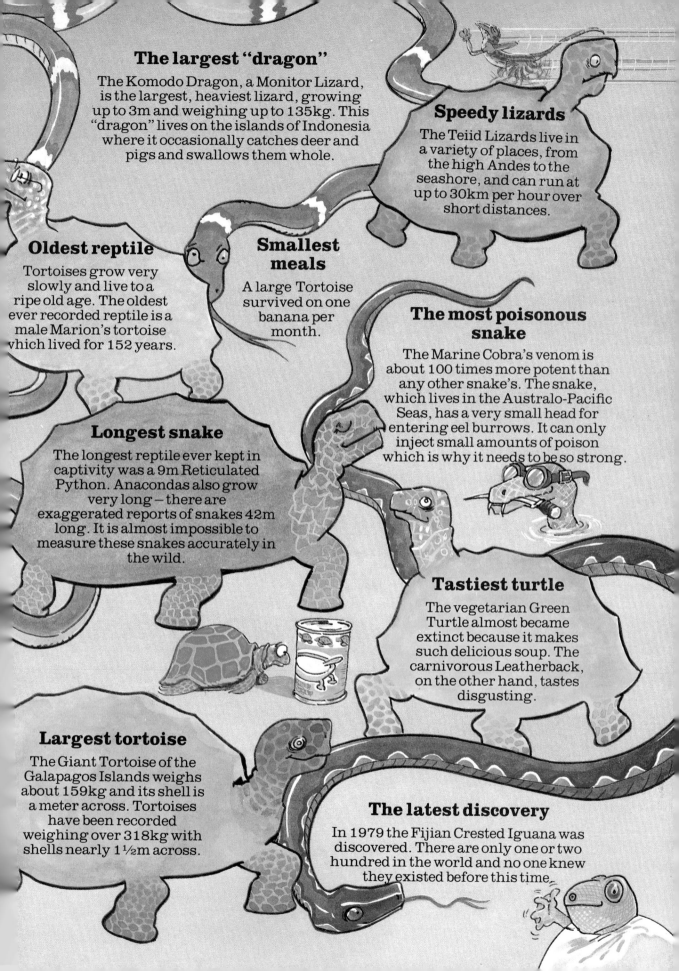

The largest "dragon"

The Komodo Dragon, a Monitor Lizard, is the largest, heaviest lizard, growing up to 3m and weighing up to 135kg. This "dragon" lives on the islands of Indonesia where it occasionally catches deer and pigs and swallows them whole.

Speedy lizards

The Teiid Lizards live in a variety of places, from the high Andes to the seashore, and can run at up to 30km per hour over short distances.

Oldest reptile

Tortoises grow very slowly and live to a ripe old age. The oldest ever recorded reptile is a male Marion's tortoise which lived for 152 years.

Smallest meals

A large Tortoise survived on one banana per month.

The most poisonous snake

The Marine Cobra's venom is about 100 times more potent than any other snake's. The snake, which lives in the Australo-Pacific Seas, has a very small head for entering eel burrows. It can only inject small amounts of poison which is why it needs to be so strong.

Longest snake

The longest reptile ever kept in captivity was a 9m Reticulated Python. Anacondas also grow very long — there are exaggerated reports of snakes 42m long. It is almost impossible to measure these snakes accurately in the wild.

Tastiest turtle

The vegetarian Green Turtle almost became extinct because it makes such delicious soup. The carnivorous Leatherback, on the other hand, tastes disgusting.

Largest tortoise

The Giant Tortoise of the Galapagos Islands weighs about 159kg and its shell is a meter across. Tortoises have been recorded weighing over 318kg with shells nearly 1½m across.

The latest discovery

In 1979 the Fijian Crested Iguana was discovered. There are only one or two hundred in the world and no one knew they existed before this time.

Were they true or false?

page 37 Skinks have antifreeze in their blood.
TRUE. The Water Skink of the Eastern Australian mountains emerges from its hibernation when there is still snow on the ground. Antifreeze in its blood keeps it active even when its body temperature is $-2°C$.

page 39 Cobras dance to the music of the snake charmer's pipe.
FALSE. The Cobra cannot hear the music. When its basket is opened, it rises in defence and then follows the movement of the pipe, ready to attack.

page 43 Snakes have been used as weapons of war.
TRUE. It is said that Hannibal had jars of live poisonous snakes thrown into his enemy's ships – a tactic which resulted in victory.

page 45 Chameleons turn black with rage.
PARTLY TRUE. Using its ability to change colour, the Chameleon may turn nearly black when faced by an enemy.

page 47 Crocodiles pretend to be logs to escape from enemies.
FALSE. The crocodile does look like a log but this is to stalk its prey.

page 50 Boas tickle their mates.
TRUE. Boas have spurs which are all that remain of back legs. The male uses his to scratch and tickle the female during courtship.

page 53 Compost heaps make good nurseries.
TRUE. Grass Snakes seek warm, moist places to lay their eggs – a compost heap is ideal.

page 54 Crocodiles climb trees.
TRUE. Young crocodiles are good climbers and often rest on branches near water.

page 57 Crocodiles cry when eating their victims.
FALSE. Saltwater Crocodiles are often seen to cry on land, but this is to rid themselves of excess salt, not remorse.

page 58 Alligators live in sewers.
PARTLY TRUE. There are reports of alligators in the sewers beneath Manhatten Island, U.S.A. These were probably pets, released into drains when their owners became bored with them.

page 61 Snakes can jump a meter high.
TRUE. A Viper of Central America can leap up to 1m to strike at its prey.

Further reading

Spotter's Guide to Dinosaurs & Other Prehistoric Animals, D. Norman (Usborne)
Spotter's Guide to Zoo Animals, R. Kidman Cox (Usborne)
Discovering Life on Earth, D. Attenborough (Collins)
Wild, Wild World of Animals: Reptiles and Amphibians, R. Oulahan (Time-Life)
Encyclopedia of Reptiles, Amphibians and Other Cold-blooded Animals (Octopus)
The Reptiles, A. Carr (Life Nature Library)
Grzimek's Animal Life Encyclopedia, Volume 6 Reptiles (Van Nostrand Reinhold)
Vanishing Species (Time Life Books)
Tortoises & Turtles, J. L. Cloudsley-Thompson (Bodley Head)
Crocodiles & Alligators, J. L. Cloudsley-Thompson (Bodley Head)
Snakes and Lizards, E. & C. Turner (Priory Press)
Strangest Creatures of the World, G. Kensinger (Ridge Press)

The Venomous Animals, R. Caras (Barre/Westover)
Venomous Animals, R. Burton (Colour Library International)
Colour for Survival, P. Ward (Orbis)
Keeping a Terrarium, S. Schmitz (Lutterworth Press)
Snakes – A Natural History, H.W. Parker & A.G.C. Grandison (British Museum)
The Hunters, P. Whitfield (Hamlyn)
The Fascination of Reptiles, M. Richardson (Andre Deutsch)
Biology of Reptiles, I. Spellerberg (Blackie)
Weird & Wonderful Wildlife, M. Marten et al (Secker & Warburg)
Poisonous Snakes, T. Phelps (Blandford Press)
Introducing Snakes, V.J. Stanek (Golden Pleasure Books)
Reptiles, A. Bellairs and J. Attridge (Hutchinson)
The World of Reptiles, A. Bellairs and R. Carrington (Chatto and Windus)

PART 3

MYSTERIES & MARVELS
OF
BIRD LIFE

Ian Wallace, Rob Hume and Rick Morris

Edited by Rick Morris
with Marit McKerchar

Designed by Teresa Foster,
Anne Sharples, Sally Godfrey,
Lesley Davey and Polly Dawes

Illustrated by David Quinn,
Alan Harris, David Mead,
Wayne Ford and Ian Jackson

Cartoons by John Shackell

Contents

The Quetzal, from Central America, was worshipped by the Aztecs as "the god of the air".

To avoid damaging his long feather train, the male drops backwards off his perch before flying away. When he sits on the eggs the train pokes up to 30 cm out of the nest hole.

The colourful but balding King Vulture from the rainforests of Central and South America. It is probably one of the few birds to find its food by smell.

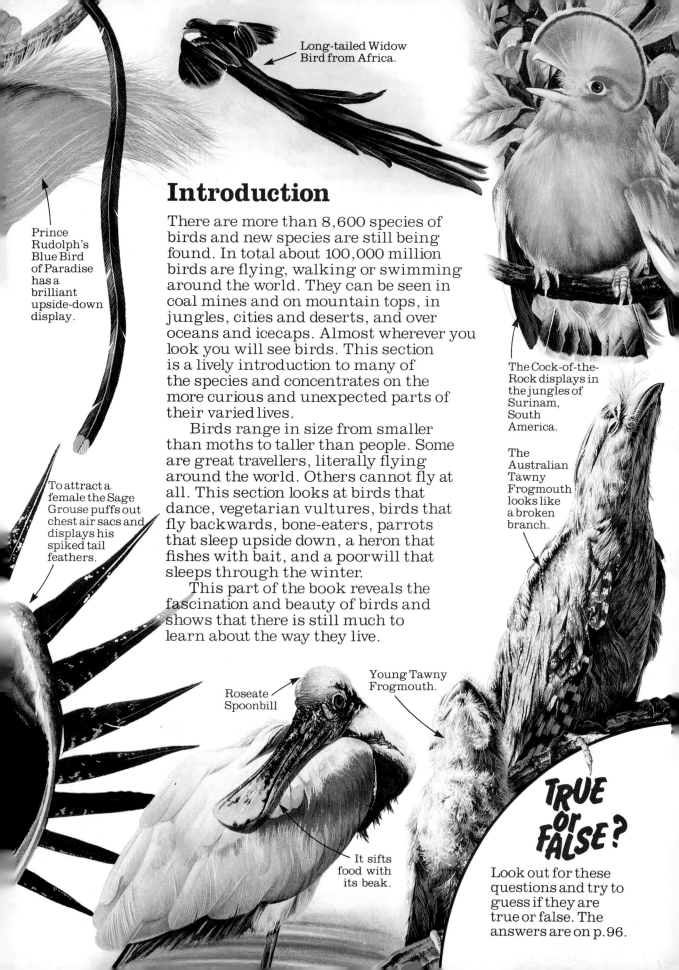

Long-tailed Widow
Bird from Africa.

Prince
Rudolph's
Blue Bird
of Paradise
has a
brilliant
upside-down
display.

Introduction

There are more than 8,600 species of
birds and new species are still being
found. In total about 100,000 million
birds are flying, walking or swimming
around the world. They can be seen in
coal mines and on mountain tops, in
jungles, cities and deserts, and over
oceans and icecaps. Almost wherever you
look you will see birds. This section
is a lively introduction to many of
the species and concentrates on the
more curious and unexpected parts of
their varied lives.

    Birds range in size from smaller
than moths to taller than people. Some
are great travellers, literally flying
around the world. Others cannot fly at
all. This section looks at birds that
dance, vegetarian vultures, birds that
fly backwards, bone-eaters, parrots
that sleep upside down, a heron that
fishes with bait, and a poorwill that
sleeps through the winter.

    This part of the book reveals the
fascination and beauty of birds and
shows that there is still much to
learn about the way they live.

To attract a
female the Sage
Grouse puffs out
chest air sacs and
displays his
spiked tail
feathers.

The Cock-of-the-
Rock displays in
the jungles of
Surinam,
South
America.

The
Australian
Tawny
Frogmouth
looks like
a broken
branch.

Roseate
Spoonbill

Young Tawny
Frogmouth.

It sifts
food with
its beak.

TRUE or FALSE?

Look out for these
questions and try to
guess if they are
true or false. The
answers are on p.96.

Fabulous feathers

Birds are not the only animals which fly – bats and insects also do. But birds are the only animals with feathers. Feathers keep them warm and help them to stay up in the air. Their colours may be used in courtship or as camouflage.

Brown tip in autumn.

Worn feather in spring.

Autumn

Spring

Male Black Lark of Asia

Turning black ▶

The wear on feathers can change a bird's colours. In his new autumn plumage, the male Black Lark of Asia is mottled brown. As wear removes the feathers' pale brown tips, black patches appear. By the spring, he is totally jet black and ready to court a female.

Long ones ▶

Many birds grow long feathers on their head, tail or wings.

When displaying to females, the King of Saxony Bird of Paradise raises his two head plumes and bounces about on branches.

Each plume is 60 cm long.

Male King of Saxony Bird of Paradise

African Snipe "drumming".

◀ Musical feathers

The African Snipe dives steeply through the air when he displays over his breeding site. As he dives, he makes a bleating "hoo-oo-oo-oo-oo-oo-ooh" sound, known as "drumming". This noise is produced by the air passing through stiff tail feathers which are spread out on each side.

Ruby-throated Hummingbird

Feather facts

The Whistling Swan has over 25,000 feathers. The much smaller Pied-billed Grebe has far denser plumage, with 15,000 feathers. The tiny Ruby-throated Hummingbird has only 940 but still has more feathers per square centimetre than the swan.

Whistling Swan

Pied-billed Grebe

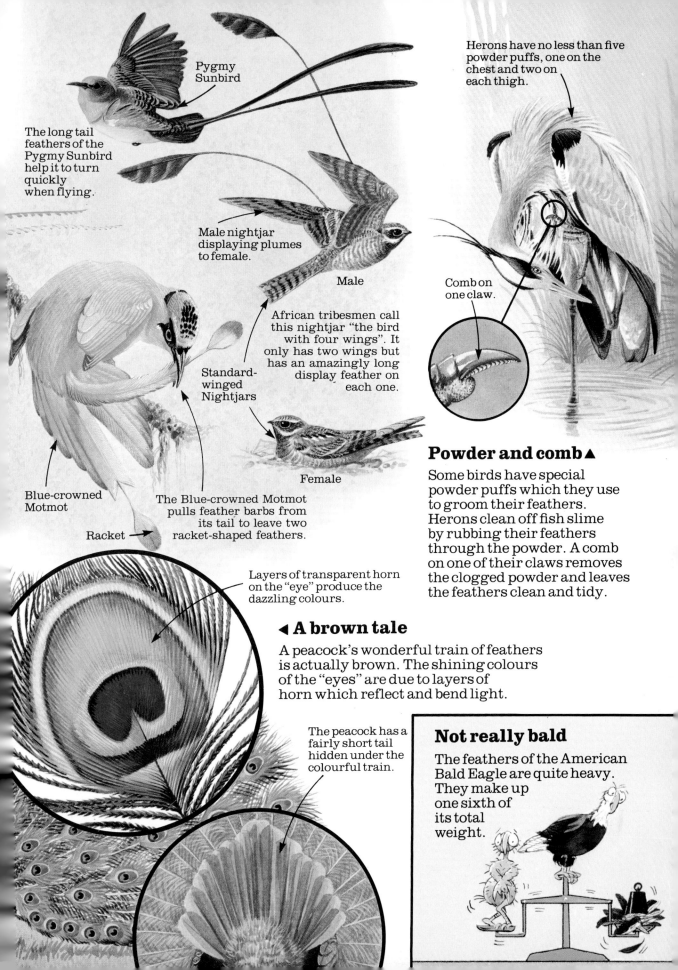

Pygmy Sunbird

The long tail feathers of the Pygmy Sunbird help it to turn quickly when flying.

Herons have no less than five powder puffs, one on the chest and two on each thigh.

Male nightjar displaying plumes to female.

Male

African tribesmen call this nightjar "the bird with four wings". It only has two wings but has an amazingly long display feather on each one.

Standard-winged Nightjars

Comb on one claw.

Female

Blue-crowned Motmot

Racket

The Blue-crowned Motmot pulls feather barbs from its tail to leave two racket-shaped feathers.

Powder and comb ▲

Some birds have special powder puffs which they use to groom their feathers. Herons clean off fish slime by rubbing their feathers through the powder. A comb on one of their claws removes the clogged powder and leaves the feathers clean and tidy.

Layers of transparent horn on the "eye" produce the dazzling colours.

◀ A brown tale

A peacock's wonderful train of feathers is actually brown. The shining colours of the "eyes" are due to layers of horn which reflect and bend light.

The peacock has a fairly short tail hidden under the colourful train.

Not really bald

The feathers of the American Bald Eagle are quite heavy. They make up one sixth of its total weight.

Eating out

Birds have no hands, so they have to find
their food with their beaks and feet.

Fishing bait ▶

Most herons wait patiently to catch fish
but the Green Heron uses bait to attract
them. It creeps to the water's edge with an
insect caught for the purpose and drops it
into the water. It then waits, completely
still, for small fish to come to the bait.
If the insect drifts away, the heron
fetches it and puts it back in position.

Green
Heron

Placing the insect . . .

. . . waiting . . .

The top of the bill
is 5 cm long.

Chisel and spear ▶

A honeycreeper from
Hawaii, the Akiapolaau,
has a unique bill for
finding food in the wood
of dead trees. The top
of the bill is long and
curved, and the bird
lifts this up while
using the shorter,
chisel-like bottom to
pound into the tree. It
spears the disturbed
insects and larvae with
the top of the bill.

. . . and a swift strike of the bill
catches the fish.

The Limpkin even feeds
snails to its young.

The Everglades
Kite feeds
only on snails.

Snail snacks

A water snail of the Florida swamps is
the speciality of two birds. The Limpkin,
with its long legs and bill, wades after
snails, searching for them on underwater
plants. The Everglades Kite – an odd bird
of prey – must wait for the snails to
come near the surface in the cool of the
day. The kite snatches them up with its
feet and flies to a branch. Its hooked
beak prises the snail from the shell.

TRUE
or
FALSE?

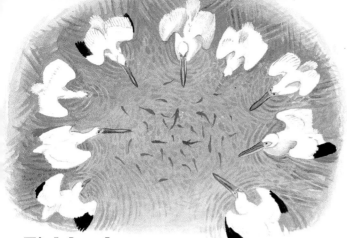

White Pelicans

The huge pouch makes an excellent fishing net. It shrinks to squeeze out the water before the fish is swallowed.

Fish herders▲

Up to 40 White Pelicans gather together in a horseshoe formation to "herd" fish into shallow water. Beating their wings and feet, they drive the fish before them. Every 15-20 seconds, as though at a signal, they plunge their bills into the centre of the arc and scoop up the trapped fish. About one in every five plunges is successful. Each pelican eats roughly 1,200 grammes of fish a day.

A nutty larder▼

The Acorn Woodpecker lives in small flocks in American oak woods. It harvests acorns and, if available, almonds and walnuts as well. In autumn it stores the nuts tightly in holes in the trees – so tightly that squirrels cannot pull them out. The woodpecker drills the holes with its beak and will re-use them year after year. The stored acorns are emergency winter food for the little 20-24 cm woodpecker.

Teaspoon effect

Grey Phalarope

To create whirlpools, the Grey Phalarope swims in tight circles and spins its body around. This has the same effect as stirring coffee with a teaspoon. Small animals in the water are probably drawn into the centre of the whirlpool where the phalarope can catch them.

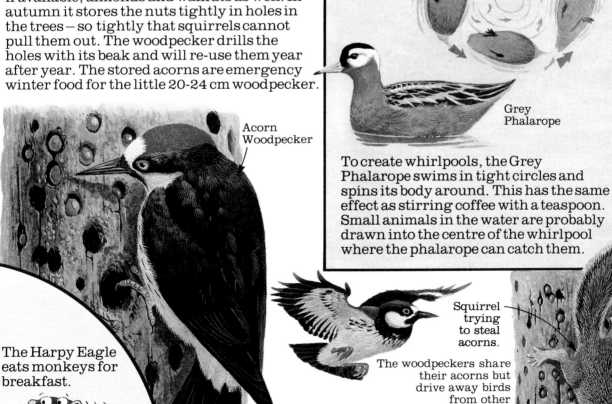

Acorn Woodpecker

The Harpy Eagle eats monkeys for breakfast.

Squirrel trying to steal acorns.

The woodpeckers share their acorns but drive away birds from other flocks.

On mild days it catches insects in mid-air – most unusual for a woodpecker.

Pirates and scavengers

Most birds find their own food but some have ways of stealing it from others. Birds are also good scavengers and are always on the lookout for an easy meal.

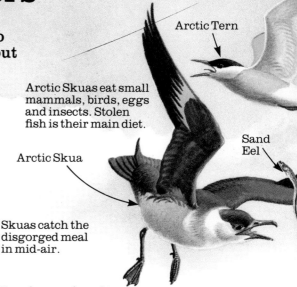

Arctic Tern

Arctic Skuas eat small mammals, birds, eggs and insects. Stolen fish is their main diet.

Arctic Skua

Sand Eel

Skuas catch the disgorged meal in mid-air.

The early bird . . .

Flocks of Lapwings and Golden Plovers feed together on worms they pull from the ground. Black-headed Gulls join these flocks and steal the worms if they can. Lapwings are the gulls' favourite targets because they take longer to pull out the worms and are less agile when chased.

The gulls may repay the plovers by warning them of predators.

Black-headed Gull

Golden Plover

Lapwing

Marine pirates ▲▼

The Arctic Skua is a graceful pirate which chases other seabirds to make them disgorge their catch of fish. The speed and agility of a pair of skuas when pursuing a gull or tern is amazing. In areas where the large Great Skua is common, the smaller Arctic Skua chases Arctic Terns, Kittiwakes and Puffins, while the Great Skua goes after Guillemots, Razorbills, Puffins and Gannets.

The Great Skua also pounces on seagulls, drowning them, and steals seabird chicks.

Truly Magnificent Frigatebird ▼

The Magnificent Frigatebird is a master of the air. It has huge, long wings and a long tail which it uses as a rudder and brake. It never settles on water and is clumsy on land but in the air it is a wonderful flier. Frigatebirds catch flying fish above the waves and feed on young turtles on beaches and fish disgorged by frightened boobies which they chase unmercifully. The way they chase these relatives of the Gannet was described in the log kept by Christopher Columbus.

Female

Male

Magnificent Frigatebird catching a flying fish.

Magnificent Frigatebird chasing a White Booby.

Arctic Skuas will fiercely attack people who come near the nest.

Lammergeier

Ant antics

As columns of army ants march through the forests of South America, they flush out insects, frogs and small mammals. The White-fronted Antbird follows the ant "armies", preying on the escaping creatures. The birds rarely eat the ants.

Bone breakers ▲

One vulture, the Lammergeier, has learnt to dispose of skeletons. It picks up a bone, flies very high with it and then drops it on to hard, flat rocks. The vulture eats the bone marrow from the broken pieces or, amazingly, swallows bits of bone. The White-necked Raven also drops bones but often gets its aim wrong and they fall on to grass.

Eye in the sky ▶

Eiders, Mergansers, Smews and other diving ducks are often watched by Herring Gulls. When they bring up fish and shell-fish, the gulls steal it if they can.

A patrolling Herring Gull, keeping an eye on the ducks.

Female

Male

Eiders diving for mussels. They can dive for over a minute to depths of 20 metres.

TRUE or FALSE?

After bathing, Starlings dry themselves on sheep.

73

Staking a claim

To breed successfully, birds need a safe place to build their nests, freedom from disturbance and a good supply of food. They may need to compete with other members of their own species for a suitable territory.

A reserved table ▼

Shelducks defend a breeding territory and the male also keeps a feeding territory nearby. The female feeds here unchallenged during the brief times she leaves the eggs. When the young hatch, they are led to this feeding area which is already free of other Shelducks who would compete for food.

As the sexes look alike, the male relies on song and display to get the right response from a female.

Robins' summer areas.

breeding territories

nest

winter

feeding

Robins' winter territories are smaller.

Female with her ducklings.

The nest may be some way from the shore, in an old rabbit burrow.

Male Shelduck

◄ Seeing red

The Robin's song can be heard clearly all around its territory. This saves it a lot of work patrolling the boundary. In spring, the male's song warns off other males but attracts females. The sight of a red breast on his territory sends the male into a fury. He attacks other males, or sometimes his own reflection or even a red rag hung in a tree.

breeding territories

feeding

river

Shelduck territories defended by the male.

island

Non-defended feeding area

Australian Gannets

breeding areas

Gannets nest on cliffs and islands.

◄ Sharing things

Gannets feed on fish in the sea. There is no point in having an individual feeding territory because they actually benefit from being in flocks, tiring out the fish by diving and chasing. Thousands of Gannets nest together and keep only a tiny territory — as far as a sitting bird can reach — around each nest.

TRUE or FALSE?

Bellbirds chime together.

Wedge-tailed
Eagles

The eagles fight
in mid-air and
on the ground.

▲ Fighting eagles

Eagles hunt over huge
areas and only defend a
small area around the nest
from other eagles. The
great Wedge-tailed Eagle
of Australia, however,
fights to keep strange
eagles out of its whole area.
Eagles may fall to the
ground and be locked in
battle for up to half an
hour. To help avoid such
fights, the eagle performs
territorial displays to
"warn off" the intruder.

The defending eagle soars through
the air performing aerobatics.

Male and
female
displaying.

Woodpeckers
know their mate's and
neighbour's drumming and
recognise intruders.

Pileated Woodpecker

Drumming
accents ▶

Woodpeckers do not
sing to mark their
territory, but they
drum their beaks against
a tree to produce a loud,
rapid rattle. The birds
can hear enough difference
in the speed and rhythm to
recognise each other.

The Great Grey Owl of northern
Europe and North America has
a wingspan of 150 cm.

Fearsome defender ▲

The Great Grey Owl defends its nest and
young fearlessly. It will attack
human intruders and can cause serious
wounds. Some skuas, eagles and
other owls also attack people in
defence of their nest.

Wooing a mate

All birds have a strong urge to breed. Finding a fit and loyal mate is all important. Generally the male advertises himself with a song, a loud call or bright plumage to attract a female.

Sunbittern showing hidden markings

Turning it on ▶

These striking birds are males trying to impress females. Some, such as Temminck's Tragopan, grow special feathers or fleshy skin for the breeding season. Others reveal hidden markings in their wings.

Count Raggi's Bird of Paradise males.

Horns

Temminck's Tragopan — the horns and wattle are colourful flesh which expands.

Wattle

◀ Brilliant display

Up to ten males of Count Raggi's Bird of Paradise display together in a tree. Each one clears away leaves that might block out the sun and defends his perch. Loud calls and bright, shimmering feathers attract a drab female. She chooses the male with the most dazzling plumage and most dramatic display. This top bird will mate with many females but the other males will probably not mate at all.

Temminck's Tragopan is a Chinese pheasant.

◀ Come into my bower

In Australia and New Guinea, male bowerbirds build and decorate a bower to attract a female. Usually, the duller the bird, the more elaborate and decorative his bower. Some collect snail shells or whitened bones, or anything blue, such as flowers, feathers and berries. When the female arrives, the male dances. She inspects him and his bower and they mate. She then builds her nest and rears the chicks on her own.

The Satin Bowerbird paints the inside of his bower with the blue juices from berries, using bark as a paintbrush.

Over 500 bones and 300 snail shells were found on the dance floor of one bower.

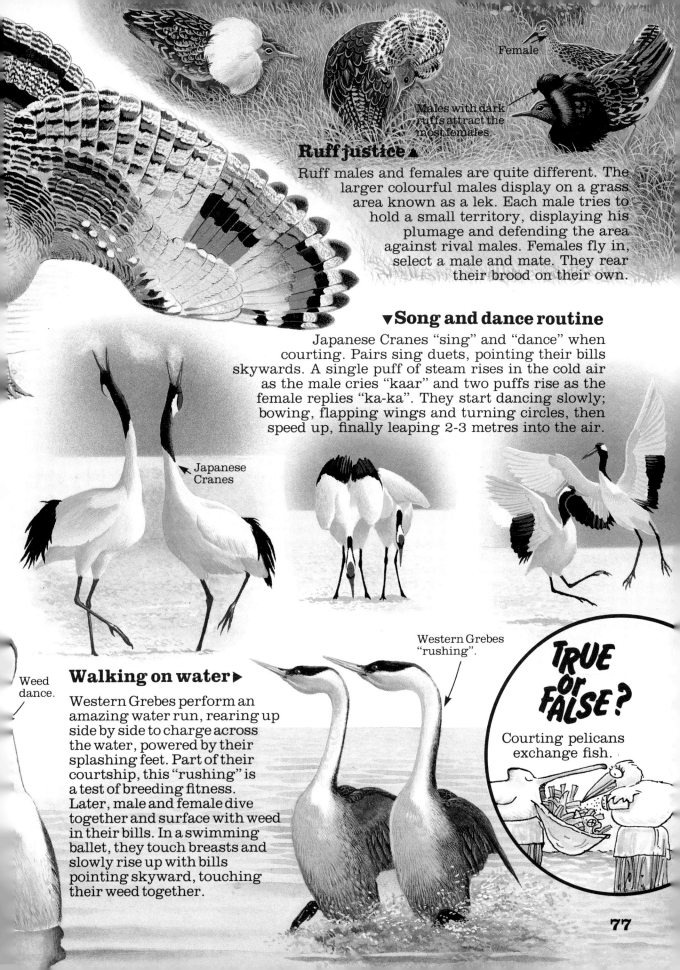

Ruff justice ▲

Ruff males and females are quite different. The larger colourful males display on a grass area known as a lek. Each male tries to hold a small territory, displaying his plumage and defending the area against rival males. Females fly in, select a male and mate. They rear their brood on their own.

Female

Males with dark ruffs attract the most females.

▼Song and dance routine

Japanese Cranes "sing" and "dance" when courting. Pairs sing duets, pointing their bills skywards. A single puff of steam rises in the cold air as the male cries "kaar" and two puffs rise as the female replies "ka-ka". They start dancing slowly; bowing, flapping wings and turning circles, then speed up, finally leaping 2-3 metres into the air.

Japanese Cranes

Western Grebes "rushing".

Weed dance.

Walking on water ▶

Western Grebes perform an amazing water run, rearing up side by side to charge across the water, powered by their splashing feet. Part of their courtship, this "rushing" is a test of breeding fitness. Later, male and female dive together and surface with weed in their bills. In a swimming ballet, they touch breasts and slowly rise up with bills pointing skyward, touching their weed together.

TRUE or FALSE?

Courting pelicans exchange fish.

Setting up home

Many animals – including mammals, insects and even fish – make some sort of nest. But birds make the most amazing and varied nests to hold their eggs and young.

▼ Dad's compost nest

The Mallee Fowl's nest is the largest made by any bird. The male builds a vast mound of soil and fills the egg chambers with damp, rotting plant material. The female lays her eggs inside these chambers and the male covers them over. Like a compost heap, the plant material rots and ferments, creating enough heat to incubate the eggs. The male opens up the chambers to reduce the heat and, at night, covers them with warm sand. The young birds, which are almost fully feathered, break out of the mound on their own and may never see their parents.

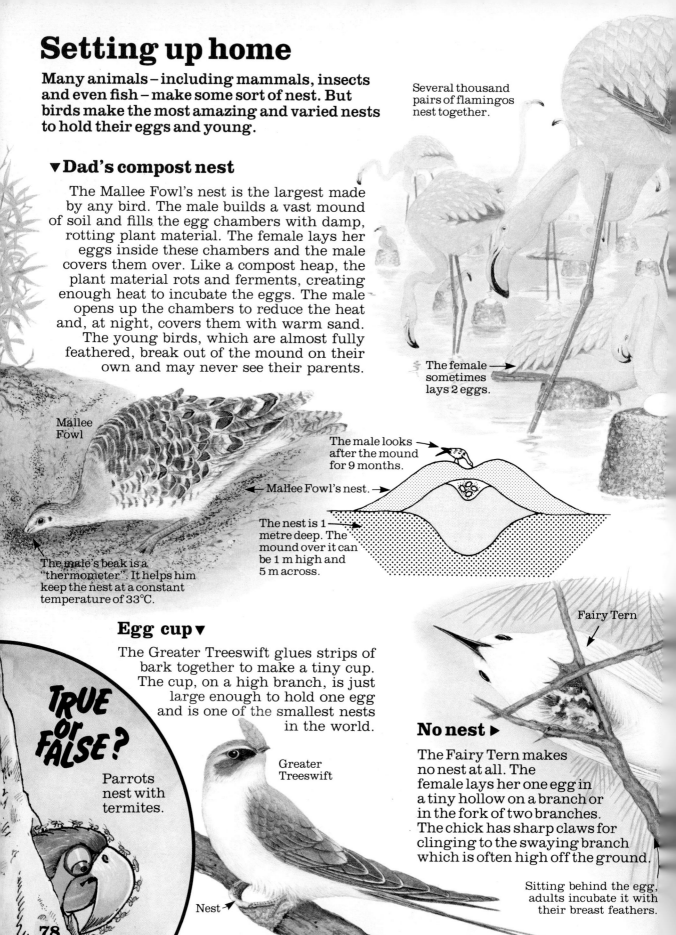

Several thousand pairs of flamingos nest together.

The female → sometimes lays 2 eggs.

Mallee Fowl

The male looks → after the mound for 9 months.

← Mallee Fowl's nest. →

The nest is 1 — metre deep. The mound over it can be 1 m high and 5 m across.

The male's beak is a "thermometer". It helps him keep the nest at a constant temperature of 33°C.

Egg cup ▼

The Greater Treeswift glues strips of bark together to make a tiny cup. The cup, on a high branch, is just large enough to hold one egg and is one of the smallest nests in the world.

Greater Treeswift

Nest →

TRUE or FALSE?

Parrots nest with termites.

Fairy Tern

No nest ▶

The Fairy Tern makes no nest at all. The female lays her one egg in a tiny hollow on a branch or in the fork of two branches. The chick has sharp claws for clinging to the swaying branch which is often high off the ground.

Sitting behind the egg, adults incubate it with their breast feathers.

Upstairs, downstairs ▶

The Hammerhead's nest may be up to 2 metres across. It is solidly built of sticks, has a high domed roof and three chambers. The highest and safest from flooding when the nest is low over a river, has three to five eggs. The young soon grow too big and move to the middle chamber. The lowest chamber is an entrance "hall".

Rufous Ovenbird

Hammerhead shooting into the tiny entrance with closed wings.

Building the nest may take six months.

◀ Well done

The ovenbirds get their name from their nests, many of which look like native mud ovens. One species builds an extraordinary 3-metre high "block of flats" with several entrances. The Rufous Ovenbird builds a strong mud nest, often perched on top of a fence post. The nest has an entrance tunnel and a separate nesting chamber. It weighs about 9 kg.

Nesting chamber

Tunnel entrance

◀ Mud mounds

Flamingos nest in colonies near lakes. Their nests are mounds of mud 40 cm across and up to 45 cm high, with a hollow scoop for the egg at the top. This gave rise to many strange ideas of how the incubating birds sat on their eggs. They actually sit on their legs with their heels poking out under their chests. The mounds last for years.

Pygmy Falcon

The straw thatch is waterproof.

A busy village ▶

Dozens of Social Weavers make a huge nest together. They build a roof in the top of a tall tree. Under this are nests of straw, each with a tunnel of stiff straws pointing downwards from a round chamber. The nests are used for roosting all the year round and may be occupied for 100 years or more. Many of the chambers may be taken over by other birds, so Social Weavers, Red-headed Finches, Lovebirds and Pygmy Falcons may all live together.

Each pair has its own entrance and nest chamber.

Rosy-Faced Lovebird

Social Weaver

Eggs to adults

Inside the egg the nervous system and heart of the young bird develop first – then the limbs, body and head, swollen by enormous eyes. When the embryo is fully developed it starts to breathe from an air space inside the shell. To get out of the egg it grows an "egg-tooth" to crack the shell.

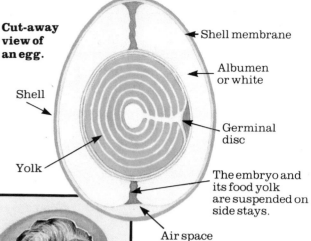

Cut-away view of an egg.

- Shell membrane
- Albumen or white
- Germinal disc
- The embryo and its food yolk are suspended on side stays.
- Air space

Shell

Yolk

Chicken's egg

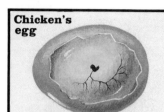  

At 3 days the chick's heart already beats. It has blood vessels.

At 15 days the chick is recognisable as a bird.

At 20 days it is fully developed and will hatch next day.

Egg care ▶

Some birds have one large patch of bare skin (a brood patch) to cover their eggs, while others have separate patches for each egg. The sitting bird leaves the eggs from time to time to stop them getting too hot. Overheating is more of a risk than the cold.

The Oystercatcher has three brood patches.

Gamebirds, gulls and waders have separate brood patches.

The eggs must be turned regularly by the parents to help the chicks develop properly. This is not easy for the Black-winged Stilt, with its long legs and long beak.

▼ Hard-working parents

Great Tit with a caterpillar for the young.

All that nestlings want is food, warmth, shelter, and more food. A pair of Great Tits visited their brood with food 10,685 times in 14 days. A female Wren fed her young 1,217 times in 16 hours.

"Hello, mum" ▶

Several days before hatching, the chick makes peeping calls from inside the egg. The hen replies, so when the chick hatches it already knows its mother's voice. Chicks which leave the nest soon after hatching quickly learn to follow their mother – she becomes "imprinted" on the chick. If they do not see their mother first, something else may become imprinted on them as "mother". Greylag Goose chicks have become attached to people in this way and one even regarded a wheelbarrow as its mother.

TRUE or FALSE?

Hungry young eaglets eat their parents.

A row of owlets ▶

Owls start incubating when the first egg is laid. The later eggs may hatch several days after the first, and the chicks will be different sizes. If the parents cannot catch enough food, the oldest, biggest chicks dominate the others and take it all. That way, one or two chicks survive, which is better than all of them having an equal share of food, and all starving at the same time.

Long-eared Owl

When there is plenty of food all the chicks survive.

Female

Unlike most birds, each female mates with several males.

Each female lays 11-18 eggs.

Male

Too many eggs

An old male Rhea may attract up to eight hens to his nest. The hens, however, will lay eggs anywhere before the nest is ready and then they will overfill it with 30 or more eggs. The cock cannot cover them all, and the hen may lay more eggs out of his reach. Since the nesting and care of the eggs and young is left entirely to the male, many of the eggs are completely wasted.

One male may incubate as many as 80 eggs.

The scientist, Konrad Lorenz, has acted as "mother" to many geese while studying their behaviour.

Canada Geese and goslings.

Nursery group ▲

Several adult Canada Geese will often look after the young of other parents. They may be in charge of dozens of goslings. Some ducks also have nursery groups of up to 100.

81

Special relationships

To find food and survive, some birds have developed special relationships with other birds, with human beings and other animals. Sometimes this works to the benefit of both but often one takes advantage of the other.

A Peregrine Falcon scaring off an Arctic Fox.

Chimango hawk

Red-breasted Geese

▼ The "cuckoo" duck

The Black-headed Duck is the only duck that copies the cuckoos and lays its eggs in other birds' nests. Unlike young cuckoos, the newly-hatched duck does not push out its companions and only shares their food for a few days before wandering off alone. The duck usually chooses water birds to foster her young but she has been known to lay her eggs in hawks' nests.

A Black-headed Duck laying her egg in a Chimango's nest in the Andes.

The Peregrine connection ▲▶

In the Arctic, Red-breasted Geese know that the presence of Peregrine Falcons means the absence of Arctic Foxes which prey on the geese and their goslings. So they nest within sight and easy reach of the falcon eyries, confident that the Peregrines will chase off the foxes. But as the numbers of falcons have declined, so have the geese.

▼ All in the family

White-fronted Bee-eaters of Kenya have a complicated social life. They nest in sand cliffs in colonies of up to 225 pairs. A male must guard his mate closely as a lone female will be quickly mobbed by other males and forced to mate. When food is scarce, dominant males force younger relatives, both male and female, to help feed their chicks. Up to a dozen birds will assist a dominant pair. When this happens, younger birds cannot breed themselves but gain experience for the next year.

Elder Sisters ▶

Sometimes young birds from a first brood will play "elder sister" to their parents' later broods. Young Moorhens often do this, looking after and feeding one or two broods of younger brothers and sisters. This probably makes them better parents.

A young Moorhen helping the adult with nest repairs.

Young Moorhen feeding a new chick.

Cattle Tyrant

Carmine Bee-eater riding on the back of a Kori Bustard.

◀▼ Easy Rider

Some birds hitch lifts on larger animals and wait for food to be provided by them. In Africa, the Carmine Bee-eater rides the huge Kori Bustard. In South America, the Cattle Tyrant sits on cows. Both watch for flying insects put up by their hosts and then capture them in the air.

TRUE or FALSE?

Blue Drongos help Chinese fishermen.

Where eagles dare ▼

Since the White-tailed Eagle has been protected, it has become less shy. Many eagles have learnt that fishermen will throw them fish scraps. Returning fishing boats are now followed by gulls, Fulmars and White-tailed Eagles.

White-tailed Eagle

Gulls

Fulmar

Arctic Fox

Colourful characters

Birds use colour in displays against rival males and to attract mates. Bright colours also attract predators, so some birds only show off their colours in display, and some are only coloured during the mating season. Females, who normally guard the eggs, are generally duller than the males, but this is not always so.

Neck cape pulled out to reveal markings.

Male Lady Amherst's Pheasant

Mating mask ▼

During the mating season, the Tufted Puffin's normally sober appearance undergoes a complete change. He wears coloured "spectacles", a brightly coloured bill, and golden head plumes like overgrown eyebrows. The Puffin uses its bill for "billing" in courtship — the male and female rub bills together.

Tufted Puffins "billing".

The Tufted Puffin is much duller in winter.

Lady's man ▲▶

Male Lady Amherst's Pheasants have a glorious plumage, as do most cock pheasants. The female, though, is a dull mottled brown which gives her excellent camouflage amongst scrub, bamboo thickets and woods. During courtship the male prances around the female, spreading his feathers to show his brilliant colours to their best advantage.

▼ Snipe's stripes

The Jack Snipe uses the stripes which run along its body to give it perfect camouflage in the marshes where it lives. When it lands, it turns its body, so that the stripes go in the same direction as the surrounding vegetation.

Jack Snipe

The bird remains quite still when its body is in the correct position.

Male frigatebird

TRUE or FALSE?

The Booby's feet are blue with cold.

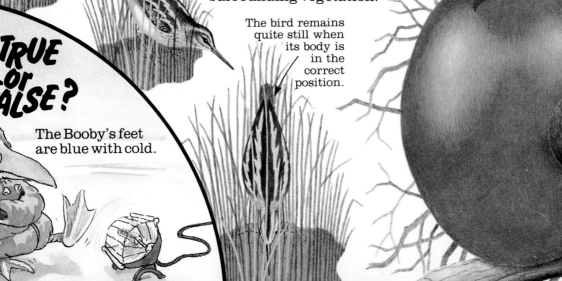

Toco Toucan

The beak is very light but strong. Serrated edges, like teeth, slice through its food.

The 23 cm beak is as long as its body.

Colour collection ▶

The Lesser Flamingo's delicate colour is thought to come from chemicals, called cartenoids, in its food. Flamingos in zoos may lose their colour if not fed on the right diet. The flamingo filters algae from the water through bristles in its bill.

Lesser Flamingo

Beautiful beaks ▲

The brilliant colours and size of the toucan's beak are a mystery. The toucan uses its beak to reach for fruit, duel with rival males and to scare small birds in order to eat their eggs, but there appears to be no reason for the beak to be quite so colourful.

▼ Fabulous females

For a long time, scientists thought that the male and female Red-lined Parrot were males of two separate species because they look so different. Both are very colourful but, surprisingly, the female is more striking than the male. In addition to the bright plumage, its noisy cries announce its presence in the jungle.

▼ Balloon bird

The male frigatebird attracts his mate with an amazing wobbly "balloon", which is an inflated throat sac. During the display he vibrates his wings and makes gobbling noises. The female shows her consent by nibbling his feathers and she rubs her head on the "balloon".

Male

Female

The Red-lined Parrot feeds on fruits, berries and nuts.

Frigatebirds nest in bushes and trees.

They live in Australia and New Guinea.

85

Migration marvels

Each spring, many birds fly from their winter grounds to summer breeding areas. Some species fly thousands of kilometres on this migration. After breeding they return to their winter areas where the food supply will be more plentiful.

Bar-headed Geese

Over the top

Bar-headed Geese fly from central Asia over the Himalayas – the world's highest mountain range – to reach their winter grounds in north India and Burma. The flight takes the birds up to an amazing height of 8,000 m – almost as high as cruising jet planes.

Moon and mud myths ▶

Before scientists discovered the facts of bird migration, people had some amazing ideas to explain where birds went in winter. Swallows were believed to dive into ponds and sleep in the mud at the bottom until spring. Some people thought birds went to the moon. Others thought small birds, like Goldcrests, hitched lifts on large birds such as storks.

Having left its breeding areas around the Bering Straits, there are few places to stop before the bird reaches the Hawaiian islands.

Bristle-thighed Curlews

Dots in the ocean ▶

The accuracy of some migrations is astonishing. For millions of years, Bristle-thighed Curlews from Alaska have wintered about 9,000 km away on tiny islands in the Pacific Ocean. To reach Hawaii or Tahiti they fly south on a bearing of 170°, continually altering course to allow for winds which drift them off target.

Migration mystery

House Martins are common summer breeders in Europe but where do they go in winter? They winter in Africa but no one is quite sure where. Many thousands have been ringed in the UK but so far only one has been recovered. In 1984 a ringed House Martin was found in Nigeria. Do all UK House Martins winter in Nigeria?

House Martins from European countries seem to winter in different parts of Africa. Birds from Germany have been found in Uganda.

Fast flight ▲

A Knot ringed in England took only eight days to reach Liberia, 5,600 km away. Its average speed was 29 km/h.

African Fish Eagle

Tawny Eagle

Social seasons ▶

The Turtle Dove is common in the woods and farmlands of Europe in summer. In winter it travels to Africa and roosts in huge flocks. One roost was shared with 50 Tawny Eagles, 15 Fish Eagles and hundreds of Black Kites – strange company for a bird whose summer neighbours are Chaffinches and Blackbirds.

Black Kites

Turtle Doves

Its temperature drops to 13°C and its heart beats very slowly.

The Poorwill crawls into a sheltered hole, fluffs out its feathers, and settles for a long, deep sleep.

Deep sleep

The Poorwill of western North America stays put during the winter months. It copes with the hardest months, when food is scarce, by hibernating. (The Trilling Nighthawk is the only other bird found hibernating.) Before hibernating, it builds up a store of fat which it can live on. About 10 grams of fat is enough "fuel" for 100 days.

It eats as much as possible before going to sleep.

The ultimate fliers

Most birds fly and are great masters of the air. Their powers of flight are matched only by the finest of the insect fliers.

The 9 cm-long Ruby-throated Hummingbird migrates over 3,000 km. 800 km is over the Gulf of Mexico.

World's worst flier?

The tinamou flies off at breakneck speed but lacks control and may kill itself by crashing headlong into a tree. Speed soon exhausts it and, if flushed from its perch several times, it can become too tired to fly. Tinamous have been seen to dash half way across a river and then flutter down to the water, tired out. Fortunately, they swim quite well and so may reach the bank. Even when running, these birds sometimes stumble and fall.

The tiniest ◄ helicopter

Hummingbirds are not only quick and agile in forward flight, they can fly up, down, sideways, backwards and upside down. As well as this, they can hover perfectly, keeping their bills quite still as they suck nectar from flowers. Their narrow wings beat 20-50 times a second and one species has been recorded at 90 beats a second. The Bee Hummingbird (males are only 57mm long) is smaller and lighter than some hawk moths.

Hovering

Swift flowing ►

Great Dusky Swifts nest and roost on cliffs behind waterfalls and must fly through sheets of falling water. Occasionally they are swept away by a sudden torrent but usually manage to struggle free.

Swept-back wings and a torpedo-shaped body are a superb design for speed.

Great Dusky Swift

Flying backwards

Beginning to roll

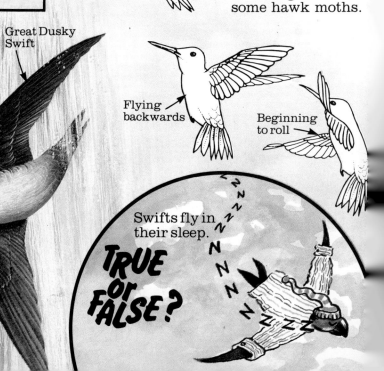

Swifts fly in their sleep.

TRUE or FALSE?

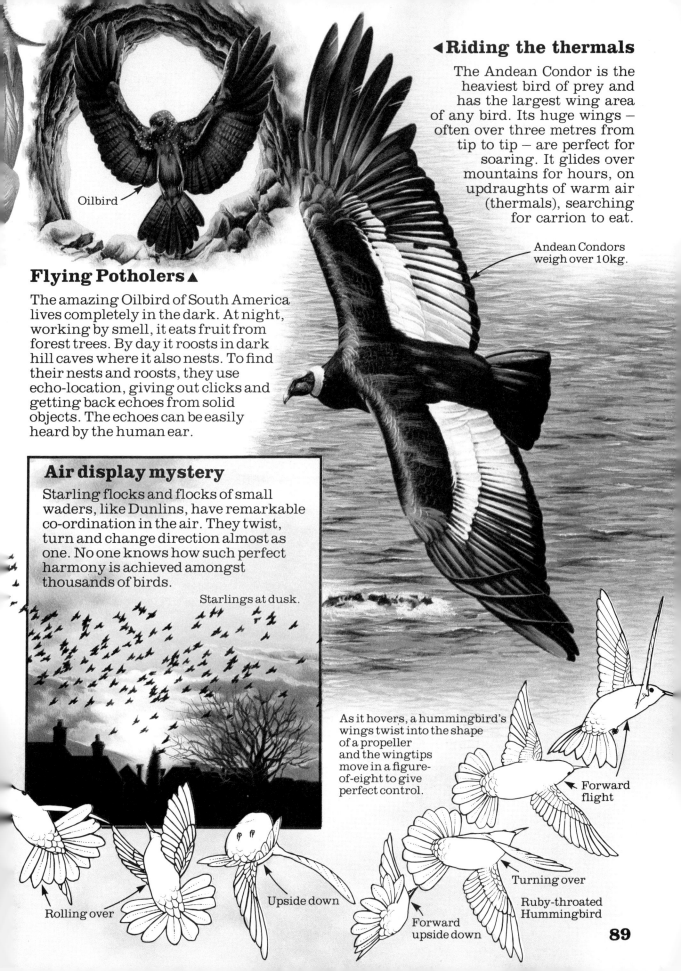

◄Riding the thermals

The Andean Condor is the heaviest bird of prey and has the largest wing area of any bird. Its huge wings — often over three metres from tip to tip — are perfect for soaring. It glides over mountains for hours, on updraughts of warm air (thermals), searching for carrion to eat.

Andean Condors weigh over 10kg.

Oilbird

Flying Potholers▲

The amazing Oilbird of South America lives completely in the dark. At night, working by smell, it eats fruit from forest trees. By day it roosts in dark hill caves where it also nests. To find their nests and roosts, they use echo-location, giving out clicks and getting back echoes from solid objects. The echoes can be easily heard by the human ear.

Air display mystery

Starling flocks and flocks of small waders, like Dunlins, have remarkable co-ordination in the air. They twist, turn and change direction almost as one. No one knows how such perfect harmony is achieved amongst thousands of birds.

Starlings at dusk.

As it hovers, a hummingbird's wings twist into the shape of a propeller and the wingtips move in a figure-of-eight to give perfect control.

Forward flight

Rolling over

Upside down

Forward upside down

Turning over

Ruby-throated Hummingbird

Sprints and marathons

As well as flying, most birds walk, run or hop. Those which depend most on their legs and feet are the ones which have lost the power to fly. Feet are also a source of power for waterbirds.

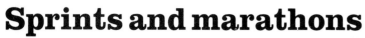

Running on water ▶

No bird can actually walk on water but the African Jacana comes close. With toes and claws up to eight centimetres long, it can stalk or sprint over thinly scattered marsh plants with no risk of sinking. Its other name is Lily-trotter.

The African Jacana can fly, swim or dive if it has to.

Ostriches have been trained to herd sheep and to scare birds from crops.

Adelie Penguins

Greater Roadrunner

Running circles around a rattlesnake, the Roadrunner darts in and out, dodging the fangs and tiring out the snake.

At the right moment, it dashes in and hammers its bill against the snake's head to kill it.

◀ Beep, beep! ▼

The Roadrunner of North America is a member of the cuckoo family. It is a poor flier and is best on the ground, running long distances, sprinting, zigzagging and darting nimbly between obstacles. It reaches speeds of 40 km/h, and is faster than any Olympic athlete. A cunning hunter, it will sprint out of cover and catch swifts flying down to drink from desert pools.

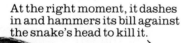

The Roadrunner swallows the dead snake whole. It may be seen running around with the snake's tail hanging from its bill.

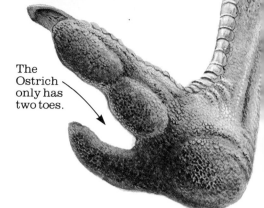

The Ostrich only has two toes.

◄ Long legs

The flightless Ostrich can be up to 2.7 metres tall with legs over 1.2 metres long. These are the longest and most powerful legs of any bird. The Ostrich can easily run at 45 km/h for 15-20 minutes and sprint at more than 70 km/h. Ostriches are nomads, joining in the game migrations of Africa to graze hundreds of kilometres of grassland.

An Ostrich's kick can kill a man.

Sanderling

◄ On its toes

All wading birds are nimble but the Sanderling moves so fast along the water's edge that it no longer grows a hind toe. It tilts forward and dashes about on its three front toes.

◄ Penguin marathons

Penguins cannot fly. To reach their Antarctic breeding grounds, Adelie Penguins waddle for up to 320 kilometres over ice floes and snow-covered rocks. When the sun is out, they march steadily in the right direction, but when it is cloudy they seem to lose their way.

Impeyan Pheasant

Snow Leopard

▲ Hill walker

All pheasants fly only short distances because they lack the normal ability of birds to quickly replace oxygen in their blood. To avoid a predator, the heavy Impeyan of the Himalayas takes off with a burst of wing beats and glides downhill. It then has to walk back up again.

Young auks →

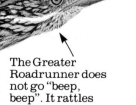

The Greater Roadrunner does not go "beep, beep". It rattles its bill to make a "clack" noise.

▲ Long-distance swimmers

Young auks, Fulmars and Gannets are too fat to fly. They crash dive into the sea from their cliff ledges and swim hundreds of kilometres towards their winter quarters. Constant paddling burns up their fat and, when they are light enough, they stagger into the air.

TRUE or FALSE?

The speedy Cassowary wears a crash helmet.

Odd birds

Male Cardinal

Fish supper ▶

Many young birds have bright orange or yellow mouths which make obvious targets for their parents to push food into. One adult bird made a mistake, and fed goldfish! A male Cardinal in North Carolina, USA, flew to the edge of a garden pool, chirped, and waited for the gaping goldfish mouths to break the surface.

The Kea calls loudly as it soars on mountain winds.

Meat-eating parrot ▲

The Kea is a fine parrot which lives near the snow line of New Zealand's mountains. It is still largely vegetarian like other parrots, but it has taken to eating carrion and is particularly fond of dead sheep. Because it has a strong, hooked beak, it was thought to be a sheep-killer and was almost wiped out by farmers. Only recent studies of its true behaviour have saved it.

The Hoatzin is also called "Stinkbird" because the contents of its crop – balls of leaves – smell awful.

◀A nutty vulture

The Palmnut Vulture – also called the Vulturine Fish Eagle – looks like normal vultures, but actually eats fruit rather than meat. Its main diet is the fleshy outsides of the African oil nut. It is the only vegetarian bird of prey.

It also eats shellfish and hunts for small fish.

◀Puzzling bird▶

The very odd Hoatzin of South America is probably related to cuckoos but its behaviour and body structure are more like a reptile than a bird in several ways. The newly-hatched Hoatzin is naked. If threatened, the young bird will jump into water to escape. It climbs up branches back to the nest, using its beak, feet and unique claws on its wrists. The claws soon disappear. The bird then grows a huge gullet (crop) to store food. Like a large reptile, the Hoatzin gorges itself with food, then has to have a long rest.

Nestlings open their mouths wide and cry for food.

Blue-crowned Hanging Parrots roosting.

Upside down ▶

Hanging parrots go to sleep hanging upside down. In this position they look like a bunch of leaves and must be very difficult for predators to spot. They sometimes hang upside down during the day and even feed upside down.

House Sparrows eating dead flies.

Flies become stuck to the radiator as the car moves along.

◀ Meals on wheels

The House Sparrow is very common in cities where it takes advantage of city life. Some House Sparrows have learnt to hop inside the engines of parked cars – they are taking flies off the radiator.

Marbled Murrelet – the small 25 cm seabird is common on the sea.

The Hoatzin is a poor flier.

Nesting mystery ▼▶

Although millions of Marbled Murrelets can be seen on the sea off Siberia and North America, almost nothing is known about their nesting habits. They are often seen flying inland with food but only three nests have been found since the first was discovered in 1931. Two nests were on rocky slopes, one in a felled tree and another, astonishingly, was 40 metres up in a fir tree. The Marbled Murrelet is probably the only auk to nest in trees. Before they can fly, the young of other auks leap from their sea-cliff nests into the sea and swim off. How young Marbled Murrelets reach the sea is a mystery.

Young Hoatzin climbing out of the water, using the unusual claws on its wings.

Record breakers

Flying giant

The Kori Bustard is probably the heaviest bird, weighing about 13-14kg and sometimes over 18kg. There have been reports of a Great Bustard even heavier than this which probably could not get off the ground.

Years in the air

The young Swift dives out of its nest in Britain for the first time and flies off to Africa. It returns to a nest site 2 or 3 years later, having covered about 72,000km – probably without ever stopping. The Sooty Tern takes off over the vast oceans and continues to fly for 3 or 4 years without ever settling on water or land.

Great birds of prey

The heaviest bird of prey is the Andean Condor, weighing up to 12kg. The Black Vulture is also very heavy. One female was reported at 12.5kg although they normally weigh less than the Condor.

Greatest span

The Wandering Albatross has the greatest wingspan of up to 3.7m from wingtip to wingtip. A Marabou was reported with an even greater wingspan of 4m, although most have a span of 2.5m.

Lighter than a moth

The tiniest birds in the world are some of the hummingbirds. The Bee Hummingbird of Cuba is only about 57mm long, half of which is beak and tail, and weighs only just over 1.5g.

Deep-sea diver

Emperor Penguins can dive down to depths of 265m, surfacing quickly again, before decompression becomes a problem.

Toughest egg

Eggs are very strong – a chicken's egg survived a 183m drop from a helicopter. An Ostrich egg will withstand the weight of an 115kg man.

Great migrations

The Arctic Tern flies 40,000km in its migration from its nesting site and back each year. The Lesser Golden Plover covers 24-27,000km in just over 6 months and flies from the Aleutians to Hawaii non-stop – 3,300km in about 1½ days with over 250,000 wingbeats.

Most ferocious bird

The most savage and efficient predators are hawks and falcons. They fly fast and when they spot their prey, swoop down and hit it hard with their outstretched talons.

Largest breeding colony

Up to 10 million Boobies and Cormorants breed together on the islands in the fish-rich currents of Peru.

Rarest bird

The Kauai e'e of Hawaii, was reduced to one pair in the world by 1980. In America, the Ivory-billed Woodpecker is nearly extinct, if not already gone for ever.

Senior citizens

A captive Andean Condor, one of the world's largest birds, lived for 72 years. In the wild, a Laysan Albatross marked with a ring, was seen alive and well at 53 years old.

Speed merchants

The Peregrine may reach speeds of about 250km per hour in long steep dives and, at this speed, a diving Golden Eagle could almost catch it. In level flight their maximum speed is 100km per hour, unless there is a following wind, and they would both be beaten by the White-throated Spinetail Swift which flies at about 171km/h.

Blurred wings

The Horned Sungem, a hummingbird, beats its wings at 90 beats per second — much faster than most hummingbirds and any other species.

The biggest swimmer

The Emperor Penguin is the biggest swimming bird, standing up to 1.2m, with a chest measurement of about 1.3m and weighing up to 42.6kg — more than twice the weight of any flying bird. The Emu is taller at nearly 2m and it swims well although it is a land bird. (Ostriches can also swim.)

Millions of birds

Of the approximately 100,000 million birds in the world, about 3,000 million are domestic chickens. The most numerous wild bird is the Red-billed Quelea of Africa — there are about 10,000 million birds.

Largest bird

The world's largest bird is the Ostrich, growing up to about 2.4m tall. Some reach 2.7m and weigh about 156kg.

The quietest bird

The Treecreeper's notes are so high and hiss-like that they can hardly be heard.

Largest egg

The Ostrich lays the largest egg — 13.5cm long, weighing 1.65kg. It is equivalent to about 18 chickens' eggs and takes about 40 minutes to soft boil!

Dizzy heights

The Alpine Chough has been recorded on Everest at 8,200m and the Lammergeier at 7,620m — both high enough to fly over the top. An airline pilot reported Whooper Swans at 8,230m, which had risen from sea level to hitch a ride from the jetstream winds.

Loudest bird

The Indian Peacock has the loudest, most far-carrying calls which echo for kilometres.

Were they true or false?

page 71 The Harpy Eagle eats monkeys for breakfast.
TRUE. The Harpy Eagle is the king of predators in South American forests. On its short, broad wings it slips easily between the trees and probably feeds largely on monkeys.

page 73 After bathing, Starlings dry themselves on sheep.
TRUE. Starlings normally dry themselves by vigorous fluttering and preening but a Starling in Shetland was seen to use the fleece of a sheep as a towel.

page 74 Bellbirds chime together.
FALSE. The Bearded Bellbird does chime like a bell but not in unison with others. It has one of the loudest calls of any bird and its metallic peal carries up to a kilometre through the South American forests.

page 77 Courting pelicans exchange fish.
FALSE. Males of many species do bring food to the female during courtship but pelicans have not been seen doing this.

page 78 Parrots nest with termites.
TRUE. Both the Hooded Parrot and the Golden-shouldered Parrot of Australia burrow into termite mounds to make their nests. They seem to live in harmony with the termites.

page 80 Hungry young eaglets eat their parents.
FALSE. Adult eagles are too strong to allow this. The oldest eaglet, however, often kills the younger eaglets and sometimes eats them.

page 83 Blue Drongos help Chinese fishermen.
FALSE. There are several drongos but not a blue one. Some Chinese fishermen use a cormorant on a lead to catch fish for them.

page 84 The Booby's feet are blue with cold.
FALSE. No one quite knows why the Blue-footed Booby's feet are blue, but it is not because of the temperature.

page 88 Swifts fly in their sleep.
TRUE. They rise high into the sky at dusk and sleep on the wing, flying down again at dawn.

page 91 The speedy Cassowary wears a crash helmet.
TRUE. The flattened horny crown on top of the head seems to act as a crash helmet as the Cassowary dashes through undergrowth in the rain forests of Australia and Papua New Guinea.

Further reading

Gone Birding, W. E. Oddie (Eyre Methuen)
Bill Oddie's Little Black Bird Book, W. E. Oddie (Eyre Methuen)
Discover Birds, D. I. M. Wallace (Whizzard Press/Andre Deutsch)
Bird Families of the World, C. J. O. Harrison (Abrams)
The Dictionary of Birds in Colour, B. Campbell (Michael Joseph/Peerage Books)
Watching Birds, D. I. M. Wallace (Usborne)
Where to Watch Birds, J. Gooders (Andre Deutsch)
Birdwatcher's Yearbook (published annually), J. E. Pemberton (Buckingham Press)
Usborne Guide to Birds of Britain and Europe, R. A. Hume (Usborne)
The Mitchell Beazley Birdwatcher's Pocket Guide, P. Hayman (Mitchell Beazley)
A Field Guide to the Birds of Britain and Europe, R. Peterson, G. Mountfort and P. A. D. Hollom (Collins)
The Birds of Britain and Europe with North Africa and the Middle East, H. Heinzel, R. Fitter and J. Parslow (Collins)
The Atlas of Breeding Birds in Britain and Ireland, J. T. R. Sharrock (T. & A. D. Poyser)
Threatened Birds of Europe, R. Hudson (Macmillan)
Birds – An Illustrated Survey of the Bird Families of the World, J. Gooders (Hamlyn)
The World Atlas of Birds, M. Bramwell (Mitchell Beazley)
Bird Life, J. Nicolai (Thames & Hudson)
The Audubon Society Field Guide to North American Birds, J. Bull and J. Farrand (Knopf)
Birds of North America – A Personal Selection, E. Porter (A & W Visual Library)
Birds and their World, J. Andrews (Hamlyn)
Every Australian Bird Illustrated, P. Wade (Rigby)
The Pictorial Encyclopedia of Birds, J. Hanzak (Hamlyn)
The Illustrated Encyclopedia of Birds, J. Hanzak and J. Formanek (Octopus)
Birds of Britain and Europe, N. Hammond and M. Everett (Pan)
A Field Guide to Australian Birds, P. Slater (Rigby)

Index

97